ONE
WHO CAME
BACK

Anita Mayer

ISBN 0 88750 382 9 (hardcover)
ISBN 0 88750 383 7 (softcover)

Cover by Bedrich Fritta
Design by Michael Macklem

Printed in Canada

PUBLISHED IN CANADA BY OBERON PRESS

For my daughters Ruth and Margi, with all my love
and thanks for their encouragement and help.

Almost two months had passed since the Allied troops had landed in Normandy. They were still advancing, though sometimes the advance seemed painfully slow. My parents, my brother Bernd and I had spent almost eighteen months in hiding. Now it was as if we could just see the light of freedom at the end of the long tunnel.

It was 2 August, 1944, a Wednesday evening, shortly after ten o'clock when a car stopped in the Korenbloemstraat near our hiding-place, the van Bebber's house. Everybody in the house, Mr. and Mrs. van Bebber, their son Jef and the nine Jewish "hiders" had gone to bed. A 10-PM curfew had been in force in the city of Tilburg for some time, so any car driving through the Korenbloemstraat after ten aroused our suspicions. We had developed a sixth sense for anything out of the ordinary, and when he heard a car that August night, my brother Bernd peered out through the blackout curtains of the second-floor front room he and I shared and said in a calm but loud voice, so everybody in the house could hear him, "They're here to get us."

In seconds, all twelve of us were downstairs in our nightclothes. The year before, in a great joint effort, we had built a complete self-maintaining shelter underneath the dining-room. All we had to do was move the dining-room table, roll back the carpet, and there was a trap door with a ladder going down into the secret room.

But we didn't have time. In the few moments it took for us to get downstairs, the doorbell rang, several times. Nobody answered as each of us tried to find a place to hide. My parents, Bernd and I ran through the kitchen and the pantry and outside into a partly open bicycle shed behind the house. We tried desperately to hide on the floor between the bicycles and pieces of wood.

Our luck had run out. Within minutes, the house was surrounded by Nazis, and we were all found and taken to the small dining-room. There we stood in our nighties and pyjamas, on top of our secret hiding-place, each of us alone with our thoughts, fears and prayers.

The Nazis, as it turned out, had come looking only for Jef van Bebber, who was wanted because of his work in the underground. We were a bonus. The van they'd brought wasn't big enough to hold us all and had to make two trips.

The van Bebber house didn't have a basement, but off the hallway was a door that led down to a small windowless cold storage. The Germans ordered four of us to wait in there, and one of them was left to guard the door. The cold storage was filled with food, and in our family, the nerves always affect the stomach. Bernd and I started to eat, cheese, apples, canned fruit; we knew from now on meals would be few and far between.

The other two watched us in dismay.

After a while, the van returned, the door was unlocked and one Nazi was assigned to guard each of us. Upstairs, mine told me I had five minutes to get dressed and pack a few things in a handbag. He checked everything I packed. I put on my black girl-guide shoes as the best to walk in, and a heavy blue sweater. Then we were loaded into the van and driven to the Tilburg police station. Some of the Dutch police who had to guard us had known us for years. They obeyed German orders but only reluctantly. The police station didn't have enough cells to accommodate all of us, so we were put into a large room at the back of the building where we slept on the floor.

The next day, Jef van Bebber was taken away to prison. That was the last time we saw him.

6

That morning, Bernd and I started to think about escaping. We knew somebody who had a warehouse close to the police station and would be willing to help us if we could only make it to his place, but before we were able to formulate a plan, we were all transported to the penitentiary in s'Hertogenbosch, about twenty kilometres away.

My mother, Jet van Leeuwen and I found ourselves in a cell meant for one person. One narrow bunk, one table and three chairs, a pail to be used as a toilet, a water carafe and a metal dish to wash ourselves in. We were supplied with some blankets so two of us could sleep on the floor. My mother was the oldest, so she slept in the bed. We got food in metal containers, handed to us by guards through a little hole in the door. The food wasn't Sunday dinner, but considering this was 1944 in the occupied Netherlands, it was adequate. Once a day we had to clean the cell. I was elected to wash the floor. It was a welcome interruption in a long day. Twice daily the heavy door was opened, and two guards came to pick us up for a ten-minute exercise. The small courtyard had heavy guardrails on top and seemed to me to be escape-proof. The guards made sure we kept on walking at all times. Several other women prisoners were exercised at the same time, and they all wanted to know what we were in for. My mother thought it was amusing to be aired with a few real toughies. On the whole it wasn't that funny. Mrs. van Leeuwen was very depressed, so all day my mother told her stories about interesting and pleasant happenings from her life.

On Sunday the families were united for half an hour. It was good to see my Dad and Bernd again. My Dad told us that he had heard we would be interrogated and advised me to be strong and determined, not to tell any more than I wanted them to know.

The next morning we were put to work. We were given pieces of paper and glue and had to fold and glue the paper into envelopes. In the afternoon a guard came to pick me up for questioning.

"Don't they want me?" my mother said to the guard.

"No, we want the girl. She will tell us more."

I was taken into an office where, behind a desk, a man in his thirties was waiting for me. He told me I looked cute in my blue-and-white striped prisoner's dress.

And a few other things to butter me up.

He asked me about Jef van Bebber and his activities with the underground. Of course I didn't know anything and politely told him so over and over again. Many times our family had gone over the things one was never going to reveal. When I wasn't co-operative, he started to yell at me.

"Do you know a Pietje Appel?"

"No. I never heard of anybody by that name."

Pietje Appel was the forged name of my cousin, Hans Badmann. He had shared our hiding-place until the day we all left the van Bebber house temporarily because of a raid on a nearby underground headquarters. When we returned, Hans had stayed on with the new family who'd taken him in. I learned the next Sunday that Hans had somehow been found and arrested and had joined the other men in jail.

I didn't tell the interrogator anything new, and he finally let me go, telling me I was too stupid to answer his questions. Neither my mother nor Jet was ever questioned.

In the next few days, we became very handy at making envelopes.

It was on Saturday that the heavy door of the cell

opened, and a guard asked us if we had room for one more woman. We said No, we had hardly enough room to sleep. The door opened a bit farther, and there before us stood my grandmother, who had been in hiding for a year and a half with one of Jef's sisters in a small village. That was too much for my mother. She broke down. My grandmother comforted her and told her she was glad to be reunited with us. I watched and asked myself, Why? Why?

On Tuesday morning, very early, a guard opened the little hole in the door and told us we'd be leaving. We should be ready in fifteen minutes. It didn't take even that to get our few belongings together.

As we left the jail, my parents were handcuffed together; so were my brother and I. The rest were also handcuffed in pairs. We were loaded into a truck and taken to the railroad station in s'Hertogenbosch, which I knew very well from my days at the Jewish High School, where I'd gone after June 1941 when we Jews were no longer allowed in the public schools. I had gone there every day on the train, which had been great fun.

Now we were taken by train to Amersfoot where we were left at the railroad station for some time, still handcuffed together. Bernd immediately started to wonder if an escape was possible. Our cousin Hans, who was handcuffed to Alex van Leeuwen, joined in our discussion. But it seemed hopeless. There were too many of the SS at the station.

So the four of us walked up and down in the August sunlight. It was eighteen months since we had been outside in the daytime. In spite of everything, at that moment it felt good to be alive. Soon the train came, and we were all ordered inside where Bernd and I, still handcuffed, sat across from our parents. Seeing the grief and despair on my father's face almost broke my heart. We had grown very close indeed in the hiding time, sharing many thoughts together and getting to know each other better than would have been possible in normal life.

We had come so close to surviving the war in hiding. The Allies were advancing steadily. Yet here we were, handcuffed, riding to an unknown destination.

z

Later the same day we arrived in Westerbork, a camp situated in the eastern part of the Netherlands. Here all the arrested Jewish people from the Netherlands were assembled. The Germans called it a Durchgangs-Lager, a transit camp. The stay in this camp varied for each individual, from a few days to years.

Now we were no longer handcuffed together; we had to walk in rows of five. We were told that first of all we had to be processed in a big wooden barrack. The processing consisted of name, birthdate, place of birth, last address, date of arrest, reason for arrest. The reason for arrest in our case seemed to be resistance to a summons (which we'd never received) to go voluntarily to a German concentration camp. The whole thing was a useless exercise of power, but the Germans were great at enumerating and cataloguing people.

Many people were being processed at this time. After going through the administration building, we had to wait in rows of five outside. While we waited, scores of Jewish prisoners crowded around us and the other new arrivals. Everyone had questions about the progress of the war and life on the outside. How long did we think the war was going to last? Were the Allies really advancing in the west? Would they reach the Netherlands soon?

We talked to acquaintances of my parents who used to live in Tilburg. They had been in Westerbork for some time and thought they would be safe, but they gave us little hope for a long stay at the camp.

There were many different reasons people stayed in Westerbork. Some were top tradesmen, electricians or plumbers. Also, the Nazis were very resourceful in the way the whole set-up to destroy the Jews was put together. When the Netherlands was first occupied, the Nazis formed a Joodse Raad, an organisation that purported to help the Jewish people but was meant only to help the Nazis locate them. Many prominent people and some of the leaders of the Jewish community donated their services. By working for the Joodse Raad, a person could get on a special list which gave him and his family the privilege of staying in Westerbork. And this was only one of the lists. There were others.

In the end, of course, the Nazis emptied Westerbork completely and shipped everybody eastward. Nevertheless a number of these people were able to survive the holocaust because they had time on their side.

As I looked around the Westerbork camp for the first time, it appeared to be a very busy place. But it was all unreal to me. I felt absolutely dissociated from it all.

After a while we were told to march in rows of five to the Straf-Barracken, the punishment barracks. Our crime, I suppose, was having tried not to end up in a place like this.

The punishment barracks consisted of two large wooden buildings, each holding between 400 and 600 people. Each was divided into two parts, one for the women and one for the men. My mother and I could stay together.

We were assigned to sleep in a sort of compound, three bunks high and three bunks wide. My mother slept on the bottom bunk and I slept on the top one. My grandmother was given one of the single beds, which stood along the walls. My father, Bernd and Hans were on the other side of the building, apparently together, but the women weren't allowed into that part of the barrack.

The next day, my mother and I were put to work outside the Straf-Barracken compound in another wooden building. Sitting at long tables with other women, we had to open and divide used batteries so the Germans could recycle them. Not a difficult job, only a dirty one.

The men of my family were working somewhere else in Westerbork. My grandmother didn't have to go outside the barracks to work, but she did have to clean up. She was always happy to see us return from work and wanted to be told everything that had happened.

Soon we started to get to know the women around us. Mother talked to those on the lower bunks and met the woman who occupied the bunk between us, Lucy Freund. On top where I was were mostly younger women and young girls. Slowly I started to introduce myself. Margot and Anne Frank were two of those who shared the top with me. Margot was the more outgoing. Anne was the serious quiet one who did very little talking, a tall pretty girl who looked very mature for her age. Their mother was in one of the lower bunks. We had all been in hiding for some time, had seen the Allies land in France and make good advances. Then almost at the last minute, when we thought we had survived the war, we were caught. Now we were sitting here amazed and bewildered.

We didn't discuss the war or what we thought would become of us. Instead we made small talk about our luxurious accommodation and, like any normal teenagers, about boys, particularly the boys in the other part of the barrack. Like the other girls, I hadn't seen any boys, except the ones I'd been in hiding with, for eighteen months. Aside from being able to spend time with my family, talking to boys was the only pleasure in Westerbork. After supper, we would stand around outside the barracks. We talked, we flirted, we promised each other things that we would do after the war was over.

Every day more people came to occupy the crowded barracks. It was hard on all of us, but it was my dear father who suffered most. He felt it was his fault we were here, though of course it wasn't. He and my mother had investigated every possible way to leave the Netherlands as far back as 1941. Only after long and careful deliberation and the friendly persuasion of Jef van Bebber, who had come to us late in 1942 on the recommendation of our friends Louis and Jet van Leeuwen, did my parents decide to go into hiding at the van Bebbers' when the time came.

It came in the early part of February 1943. The Germans in Tilburg let my parents know they wanted our house. They wanted the house with all the furniture and everything else in it. We had a few days to find accommodation with any Jewish family in Tilburg we might choose to live with.

We made arrangements with three different families. One older lady was going to take my grandmother in. My parents would be staying with another family, and for Bernd and me something was also arranged. We didn't tell the people exactly when we'd be coming, so we had enough time to disappear without anyone looking for us. At night, Jef van Bebber moved the beds, clothing, books and games we'd packed into our garage. The rest we left for the Germans. We walked out of our house for the last time at ten to six on the evening of 15 February, 1943. After having supper with the Samson family, we walked to the other end of the city, our destination the van Bebber house, where we were received with open arms and were shown every possible human kindness. My parents had made the best decision possible under the circumstances, but it was hard to convince my father of that **now**.

In our year and a half of voluntary confinement, we had lived with up to fifteen people in a relatively small house, but somehow I had been able to find a place to be alone, to have a little bit of privacy, just to think. In Westerbork one was without any kind of privacy. The hygiene in the barracks was not too great either. There were toilets next to the barracks, but little to wash up with. Some distance away were wash and shower facilities. Mother and I used to go any time we were allowed to, but never without a guard to keep an eye on us.

When I got my menstrual period, my mother went to find out if any sanitary napkins were available. Yes, one napkin a month could be obtained by each young woman.

What luxury! My mother decided to take matters into her own hands. On our next visit to the showers, she helped me take a hot shower while standing on my head. It wasn't ideal, but it served its purpose.

One day went into the next, and if any of us felt some hope, it was never enough to mention out loud.

3

It had become apparent over the years that most transports of Jewish prisoners eastward from Westerbork took place on Tuesdays. During the latter days of August, rumours reached our barracks that the next transport was leaving (for what was called an undetermined destination) on the first Tuesday in September.

Since the first day in Westerbork, we had known the day would not be far off when we would be shipped somewhere else, but we had still hoped the Allies might advance faster and maybe . . . But that was not to be.

The Allies did advance remarkably in the last days of August and the beginning of September, so much so that the Nazis decided to move up the date of the transport from Tuesday, 5 September to Sunday, 3 September.

Very early that Sunday morning, all the inhabitants of both Straf barracks were awakened and told to gather up their belongings and be ready for transport. Since the belongings were only small suitcases or handbags, it didn't involve much work to pack them. But anticipation, and the fear of what now appeared to be inevitable, took hold of us all. Everybody wanted to hold a dear one in his arms for a moment and hear or say a word of encouragement. I was almost afraid to look at my father's face, which had always had so much strength and was now filled with a deep pain. My grandmother had wise words of love and strength, and she stayed calm through it all.

We were hurried out of the barracks to be counted and counted again. My parents, my grandmother, Bernd, Hans and I tried to stay together as we marched through the Westerbork camp to the administration barracks, where we were counted again and got some useless instructions. Then 1019 human beings were loaded, like cattle on the way to a slaughterhouse, into freight cars. They were completely darkened. Every possible opening had been reinforced with extra planks. About 75 people were loaded into each car. Our family was all together, and near us was the Frank family, the van Pelz family and a young man named Zendyk. We were all sitting on the floor, more or less on top of each other. My grandmother was seated on her suitcase against the wall. Not once during the trip did she utter a complaint.

How many times had she said when we were still living in our house in Tilburg, "If I can only outlive Hitler and see his defeat."

The train ride took about 40 hours. I slept most of the time, leaning against one or another sleeping person. Some people talked and talked.

All of a sudden the train came to a halt, the doors were thrown open and we found ourselves at the platform of a railroad station, but there were no buildings and no name of the station anywhere. It was about 3 AM, 5 September. Huge orange searchlights were all around in the night. We were ordered out of the freight cars and had to assemble, women on one side, men on the other. We were surrounded by men in striped jail outfits who did not speak. They only ordered us to put down our baggage, which they said would follow.

What happened next took only a second. My mother, my grandmother and I were standing together holding hands in a row of five women. An SS man came and pushed my mother and grandmother one way and me another. I tried to look back, but I couldn't see them. I never saw them again.

I was pushed and shoved into a row with four other young women, unable to comprehend what was going on. The expression on the faces of the men in jail outfits was something I'd never seen before. I had seen people with angry, hurt and sad faces, but these faces didn't look like anything human. These were faces that seemed to be beyond any kind of human feeling. They looked as if masks had been pulled very tightly over the flesh. If they spoke, it seemed, the masks would break.

We had to walk a few hundred yards, then we had to stop. It was still dark. Only two silhouettes were visible. Two high towers with fencing. The noises travelled through the night. I could hear dogs barking and howling, then a human voice crying and then music. Again we had to walk on. The girl next to me spoke, but I couldn't answer.

We marched on a little way. On both sides of the road were high fences with a watchtower about every 25 metres.

At daybreak we found ourselves in an open space in front of a large building. Several long tables stood under a porch next to the building. Female prisoners, under the iron rule of Nazi women, were taking down our name, date of birth and so on, and all the women who were left from our transport were alphabetically tattooed. I watched in disbelief one woman stretching my skin while another one tattooed my arm. I became A 25205. The women prisoners talked to us, and we found that we were in Birkenau, a part of the big Auschwitz complex of concentration camps. Birkenau was the one with the crematoriums and gas chambers. They told us we were lucky that we were getting numbers on our arms. It meant maybe we had a chance to live. They wanted to know about the war. Did we think the Allies would ever win?

Most of us still had a purse or some of our meagre belongings in our hands, but at this point guards came up to us and grabbed every last thing. My last belongings were my glasses and my watch. Again we had to stand in rows of five to be marched into the building. In a very large room, big enough to hold 500 or more people, we were ordered to take off all our clothing except our shoes.

We didn't wake up from this bad dream. It was real.

Some women took too long to undress, and SS men came and tore the clothes off their bodies. The clothing was thrown into big open kettles of steaming hot water. The men operating these boilers stood around looking over the naked women and giving their opinions while some of the male guards were cutting the women's hair. Others were busy with long sharp razors to cut the hair from the women's underarms and pubic areas, not caring whether the knife cut into the skin. As I tried to cope with the physical pain and the pain of nakedness, I was thinking about my mother and my grandmother, wondering where they were, and about my Dad, Hans and Bernd. Hoping and praying.

One side of the room was all windows, which were open to let a cold wind blow in. The other side was terribly hot because of the boilers. We were standing in between.

After some time, we were all sent into the next room, which turned out to be a large shower-room. Our shoes had to be put on the side and we went under very hot showers. Then they turned them ice cold. Everything to make one sick.

We were in the showers for some time, and I had a chance to look around me and see the young girls and women, naked, some of them having their menstrual period, totally robbed of their dignity.

From the shower-room, we first had to run through draughty halls, and then we were given some clothing. I received one pair of underpants and a cotton dress.

We had gone through the whole building from one side to the other, and now we waited outside until everybody had received her clothing.

18

"Anita. Anita."

I hear a well-known voice, and I look behind me, and about fifteen metres from me is my brother.

His head has been shaved, and his ears stick out. We move a little closer to each other. He has his arms stretched out, his hands in fists.

"Always remember," he says, "the Nazis can hurt you from the outside but never from the inside. The war will be over in five or six weeks and I count on you and I'll see you then."

I had just enough time to ask about Dad and Hans. Hans was somewhere with him, but not Dad.

And away he went, I don't know where.

It was about 1.30 PM, Tuesday 5 September. I had seen Bernd for only a minute, but it had a lasting influence on my whole being. I straightened my back. I was going to give it a real fight. We were lined up and counted and then marched off. I started to be more conscious of the women I knew from Westerbork. I started to talk a bit. But there were too many impressions to take in, and whatever I saw gave me terrible pain, especially when I saw several mothers and daughters together. We walked the same way as in the night, but now we saw everything. The sensation of horror was confirmed. We saw men in striped outfits working as labourers, others moving from one place to another. All of them tried to talk to us, wanting to hear any kind of news from the outside world.

Where did we come from? Where were the Allies now? Would they win the war soon? They spoke many languages, but they all had the same pains and the same hopes. What they wanted to hear was that maybe, maybe, they had a small possible chance to survive this hell.

The Nazis called our group of women Die Höllander.

There were between 250 and 300 of us. Die Höllander. Nobody was permitted to speak to any other prisoners, but I told anybody who wanted to hear me that the war would be finished in five to six weeks.

We marched slowly on, seeing several camp units, all of them filled with people; one seemed to look much like the next. At last we arrived at our destination, BAIIB Frauen-Vernichtigungslager Birkenau. Vernichtigung means destroy, and that was the intention the Germans had for us. We marched through a large gate. Inside the gate was a small guard-house.

I tried to look around me. Women stood in long lines waiting to get their soup ration. We were very hungry too, but we didn't know yet what real hunger pains were.

There was pushing and shoving, and everyone tried to be first or to get a little extra, but what struck me most of all again was the absence of any facial expression on these young women. Mask-like hollow faces with close-shaven heads. All that was left was the animal drive to survive and lots of deep sorrow. Most of the inhabitants of BAIIB seemed to be women between their late teens and their early forties. I looked at them in disbelief.

"I hope I'll never be like them," I said.

When we received our portion of soup, we waited our turn, but we were watching all the tricks. Afterward we were counted again and marched through BAIIB down the road, which was called die Lager Strasse.

On both sides of the road were barracks, all looking the same from the outside, large wooden sheds. Soon we learned that most were sleeping barracks, a few were latrine barracks and the others were washing barracks. Before we were ordered into No. 27, we had to stand Appel again and be counted once more.

At the entrance to the sleeping barracks were women

with screaming, bitching voices. Inside we found wooden boxes in tiers of three. They were going to be our sleeping places. They reminded me of the feeding boxes for horses I'd seen on farms. A certain number of these boxes were for us Hollanders, but there were also some women already in the barracks from other countries.

I had no relatives, no close friends. I looked for a place to put myself. Mrs. Frank noticed me searching around and was kind enough to ask about my mother and grandmother. I told her I was alone. She asked me to join her, Margot, Anne and Mrs. van Pelz in their box. I gladly accepted.

The sleeping places were the only rest places we had. There was no place to sit down. We received a few blankets for each box but not enough to cover us all.

The latrine barracks were across the Lager Strasse from our barracks. This turned out to be dangerous. The Nazi guards might at any time, night or day, start screaming Zahl-Appel, and if you happened to be in the latrine and weren't immediately back on the other side of the road to be counted, they were waiting for you with long whips in their hands and willing to use them.

The washing barracks had long rows of cold-water taps and drains in the floor. No soap, towels, or toilet-paper, of course. At the beginning of each row of taps was a small drawing of a skeleton warning us not to drink the water because of typhus contamination. That first day, we missed the time when drinks (a sort of tea-coloured liquid) were distributed. Very thirsty, I kept looking at the skeleton and wondering.

At the back of the barracks, maybe twenty metres from the door, was the high barbed-wire fence that ran around each camp. The fences were charged with high-voltage electricity. About every hundred metres were high watchtowers manned by SS guards with machine-guns. At night blinding searchlights were turned on. The first time we came to the back of the barracks, we heard men calling us. I went closer to the fence. The men looked like the skeleton in the biology class at school, but they were still alive and speaking. They were Dutchmen who had been at Birkenau for some time. They told us matter-of-factly that they had been selected by the German camp doctors to die any day now. They had many questions to ask us, for we represented the world outside; we had seen it only a short while ago. (Yet to me the last couple of days seemed like a long long period of astonishment and agony.)

The men were mostly interested in people, their relatives and friends. Did we know this one? Did we know that one? What had happened to them? They gave us long lists of people they had known and seen perish. I wasn't able to help them much as most of the men and their friends had lived in Amsterdam. Several of the other girls knew one or two of the men and were glad to be able to answer some of their questions.

These men had nothing more to fight with or to fight for. Somehow they appeared relaxed. They had accepted their fate. Two days later they were all gone and the barracks was empty for a few days.

Our days in Auschwitz started as soon as the sun was up with a guard running through the barracks screaming at the top of his voice.

"Zahl-Appel. Schnell! Schnell!"

As we always had all our clothing on, the only thing we had to do was step into our shoes, and we were ready to stand outside the barracks in neat rows of five. We were counted and counted again. These counts were one of the main torments of the camps because they took place in the heat or cold, sun or rain. After perhaps an hour, we had to go inside the barrack and clean and scrub the place.

"Sauber! Sauber!"

The desire for clean floors was one of the Nazis' many idiosyncrasies.

Some of the women would go to the kitchen to fetch our once-a-day drinks, which were carried in large containers something like farmers use for fresh milk. Later the empties were taken back to the kitchen.

The Nazis had many jobs for us, most of them absolutely useless, but all of them invented to plague and humiliate, to break one's resistance. On the first day we had to march under heavy guard outside the BAIIB camp and around the BAIIA toward the station. There we had to carry bricks from one place to another, making sure we carried them the way they wanted us to, with our arms stretched out so they would feel heavier. I'm sure that when the Jews were slaves in Egypt they had to carry many a stone to build the pyramids; we never found out what use, if any, our bricks had.

When we passed the guard-house on our first trip outside the Lager, we were positive we saw a great map on the wall. We talked about it the whole way, and on the way back we stretched to see it again. Each of us saw something different. I thought I saw a map of Europe with little flags on different spots.

When we got back to the barracks, we got lined up and received our meal. Soup. For the amount of work we'd done, it was far too little.

The September sun was hot, and, as I looked around me, I saw several mothers and daughters standing talking to each other, giving each other encouragement and strength. Why was I standing alone? Oh, Mrs. Frank was very kind to me, and I had talked to many of the other girls and women, but why was I alone?

In the afternoon, another trip outside the camp, this time to carry sod from one place to another. Again at night we stood for a long count and then received our daily ration of bread, a piece equal to two slices of bread, with about ten grams of butter or a tiny piece of cheese. From the beginning I learned it was extremely difficult to decide what to do with the meagre portion of food, eat the bread right then and have nothing until soup the next day, or divide it between evening and morning. Whatever decision I made, my stomach was never satisfied.

During that night, I had to go to the latrine. At night one had to use a large bucket behind the barrack. As I came out, I saw a young woman throw herself against the barbed wire. She was instantly electrocuted. I stood in dismay.

"Do you want to do that too?" the guard from the watchtower yelled at me.

I rushed back into the barrack, forgetting the reason I'd gone out.

The next morning we were busy again doing tiring, irritating, useless jobs. I felt very low. After our soup, we were standing beside the barracks when the torment within me seemed to take over and a flood of tears came rolling down my face. I couldn't stop crying.

Lenie de Jong and her friend Annie took pity on me. They made me talk about what was making me cry. It was good to say it aloud. It was good to tell my friends that my brother Bernd had promised me that the war would be over in five or six weeks and that he depended on me to be there after the war. The girls told me it would work out, but I had to fight. I dried my tears and never cried again.

After the short rest period we did the same things as in the morning. We were often marched down the Lager Strasse by one bunch of guards and then another bunch came and chased us the other way with long whips. Once I felt the lash of the whip, I became extremely fast in changing directions.

Within the first few days, we learned a lot about Birkenau. Each of us talked to some of the other prisoners, from Poland, Hungary, Greece, France, Belgium. They were all eager to talk to people who had some knowledge of the latest developments in the war.

After a couple of days, I met Lucy Freund again. She was not happy where she was sleeping. Could she join me? The box I shared with the Franks, Mrs. van Pelz and many others was full. However reluctantly, I decided to leave my new friends and find a place with Mrs. Freund. She became like a mother. Her companionship was one of the best things that ever happened to me. Her deep religious belief, her down-to-earth sense of humour and her intelligence were a great comfort. We joined in a sleeping box with Lenie, Annie, Rosy, Netty Slager, Bloeme Emden and several others.

We were near the back exit of the barrack, and I remember one night I had to go out to make use of the bucket. This time the bucket was full, and from the watchtower the SS ordered me to carry it to the latrine. Under great searchlights, I carried the heavy lot through the night. Before my eyes I saw the gruesome reality of the red smoking crematorium chimneys. I smelled human flesh burning.

After three or four days in the camp, some of our girls received messages from their husbands through men who were working in BAIIB for a couple of hours. The messages were just words of encouragement and regards, but any news gave all of us a lift. I was still convinced the war would be over in five or six weeks. In the meantime, we stretched our necks every time we marched past the guard-house, trying to see if the little flags on the map had changed position.

The nights were becoming more and more unbearable for me. The closeness of the bodies, even if they were those of my friends, drove me almost mad. Going to the bucket and seeing the chimneys or hearing human cries was no escape. Then the Allies came and bombed several nights, somewhere in Auschwitz, probably some factories. That was music to my ears, a sign that the war was going on.

The days were warm, but at night it often rained, and in the corner of our bunk the rain came through the roof. Nobody wanted to be on the end and get wet. I volunteered, thinking a little wet couldn't hurt me and I'd have only one body against me during the night.

"Anita is getting a bit funny, wanting to sleep in the rain," I overheard my friends saying.

Within a week of our arrival in Birkenau, diseases started to break out. Scarlet fever was the first, and it was mostly girls about my age who were stricken with it and sent into the sick barracks. Because I'd been deadly ill with scarlet fever when I was six years old, I wasn't too concerned for myself.

After a couple of cases had been discovered, the Nazis went into action, and every second day we all had to march naked past the doctor so our bodies could be checked for spots. This was the first time I saw Dr. Mengele, who was a tall and handsome man. Each person's stomach was checked for scarlet fever, and the ones suspected were sent to the sick barracks. After a few days my throat was sore, and I didn't dare look at my stomach.

By the time of the next selection, I found a way to avoid my turn by walking nonchalantly backward and catching up with the women who had had their turn already. Next day my throat felt better again.

There was also an outbreak of dysentery, probably as a result of the drinking water. The women who were stricken with this sickness had to carry on with heavy labour all day. It was heartbreaking to see strong people deteriorate almost before one's eyes.

My thirst, which had started on the first day, grew steadily greater, but the skeletons in the washroom kept me from drinking. Soon my mouth was so dried out from working in the warm sun that I was bleeding from my mouth and lips, sometimes for several hours. A couple of evenings, I went to the washing barracks and looked at the water taps and then decided that I would try to go one more day. But finally one evening I felt so dried out and sick from thirst I took one big sip of water. The next day I found myself still alive and well. From then on I had my daily sip of forbidden water, sometimes even two sips, and each day I was surprised nothing happened to me.

Every morning now, we would ask each other which day of the week it was, the date and the Jewish date, to make sure we kept in touch with normal human thinking.

Our heavy labour continued, mostly outside our own Lager. Each time we passed the guard-house, we would try to guess where the flags were now. I kept counting the five or six weeks.

One day as we came back into our Lager from outside labour, I saw in front of me an eight- or nine-year-old girl kneeling on a hill of stones, her arms above her head, with a heavy stone in her hands, a guard with a rifle next to her. The expression on her face showed all of human pain and suffering put together. And I had to walk on.

4

The best chance we had to talk to the other women prisoners was in the latrine or the washing barracks in the early evenings. Here we learned that one of the barracks was known as the sewing-room, and it was possible to get a brassière. Well I certainly was never a girl who could go without. It didn't take us long to get more details. The girl from the sewing-room was a Polish girl who had been in Birkenau for some time. She told us we could order a bra for the next day in exchange for one day's ration of bread.

Lucy and I decided right away. We ordered one for me for the next day and paid the girl with one day's ration of bread. Lucy and I split our ration that night, and when Lucy's bra arrived we split our ration again. We never found out what and for whom the girls in the sewing-room sewed, but we didn't care; all we cared for was our new garment. Unfortunately our new-found luxury didn't last long. A few days after we bought our bras, we lost all our clothing.

The women of our group had never understood why, on arrival at Birkenau, we had only got our hair cut short while all the other women in the Frauen Vernichtigungs-lager were baldheaded. We had heard spiteful remarks from the other prisoners from the moment we entered the camp.

All this changed on the 20th of September, when shortly after the morning Appel, the "Höllander" were called for a special Appel. Under screaming, swearing and whipping, we had to march to the showers. A long walk to the building we'd started from on our first day in Birkenau. Many of my friends thought we were going to be marched to the gas chambers, but I didn't let myself have such thoughts. Nevertheless every minute of every hour had sixty seconds, and it seemed every second was used to torture us.

We entered the big hall. Our clothing was taken from us, our bodies were shaved and this time we also lost the hair on our heads. I watched the floor being covered with every colour of hair. The men used their long razors carelessly and with great pleasure. We had to stand around naked for a long time before we went to the next stop, the showers. The hot shower felt good. It had been a couple of weeks since I had felt hot water on me. Then came the cold water, no towels, just open doors and draught. Time appeared to stand still. Hardly anybody talked.

At last we were given a pair of underpants and a dress, scarcely enough clothing with the fall season starting. The early mornings and evenings had already become quite cold. We looked each other over, the clothes, the shape of our bald heads, trying very hard to get humour and reality back. Even though we couldn't see ourselves, looking at our friends was a sad sight.

The afternoon had come, and we had missed our meal of soup. The hunger pain started to take over from all the other aches. It was late in the afternoon when we were marched back to our own Lager with many angry guards breathing down our necks and using their long rubber whips. I never tried to figure out why the Germans did any of these things; I only tried to get hurt as little as possible and kept counting the days till the end of the war.

This dreadful day seemed never to end. Everybody

looked exhausted, but our feet kept on marching.

In the first week in Birkenau, I'd met, through Netty Slager, a young woman in her late twenties or early thirties. Netty had known her before the war when they'd lived in the same town, Steenwyk. We introduced ourselves. Her last name was Culp. I asked her how she spelled it.

Why was I interested in the spelling of a name in a place like this? I told her my story.

My maternal grandmother had always lived with our family, and over the years I had heard every family story from her. My grandfather Culp, who had died several years before I was born, came from a large family, and my grandmother kept in touch with most of them by writing letters and going on extended visits. What had always intrigued me when I went upstairs to my grandmother's room was her box of old letters and paraphernalia, especially a couple of letters from one of the older brothers of my grandfather. The brother had left his parents' home at a very early age, and for many years none of the family had heard from him. Then came a letter from him telling them he was fine, living somewhere in Groningen in the Netherlands with a family. He wanted to know how everybody was. I never found out what kind of impression his letter made on the family. A second letter in the box from the same brother was of a later date, and it was obviously written in answer to somebody's reply to his first letter. According to my grandmother, nobody had heard from him again.

When I finished telling her my story, the young woman said, "That lost brother from the letters was my grandfather."

We talked a bit about our families, but it wasn't the time or place for much reminiscing. Still, I had found a person who was related to me, a second cousin. She was a small, slender person; she told me she didn't think she'd be able to survive even a few weeks.

After we had returned from that second trip to the showers, she came to me to tell me that she thought her time had come. She wanted to stand in a row next to me during Appel in case she died after the ration of bread for the day had been distributed. She wanted me to have her ration before somebody else had a chance to steal it. I tried to assure her that she wouldn't die yet, but she looked very weak. Within a few minutes of receiving her ration, she fell dead. Not to be able to bend down to give the smallest expression of human compassion was almost unbearable, but it was impossible to move.

The Nazis were still not satisfied. During the Appel, the SS guards were shooting between the rows of women, explaining that they wanted to make sure that the lines we formed were absolutely straight. We had to manoeuvre our bodies forward and backward not to get hit by one of the passing bullets.

After the Appel the bodies of the people who had died were loaded on a cart and taken away.

5

After our trip to the showers, we no longer looked different from the other women, and the teasing about our beautiful hair belonged to the past. Instead I had to get used to the feeling of all kinds of weather on my bald head. In the past, we would comb our hair with our hands, as we didn't have combs, and admire each other's messy hair. Now we looked each other over, wondering whose would be the first to grow again. Would it be curly

31

or would it be straight?

There was lots of activity in Birkenau in the latter part of September. Almost daily transports of people arrived from Hungary. We would hear the commotion in the night. Those weren't the only noises we heard. The Allies were bombing somewhere in Auschwitz. That noise made the guards very nervous, and they'd start to scream. Sometimes they made us come out of our bunks and stand in a row so that we couldn't sleep through their aggravation. To me, the bombing was like hearing my favourite piece of music being played again and again. The Allies hadn't forgotten us; time was coming closer to Bernd's prediction.

But any feelings, good or bad, disappeared when I went outside at night. The fire coming out of the tall chimneys, going up with the wind on a clear night or on a cloudy night just hanging there spreading the smell of burned human bodies, paralyzed me.

The SS doctors, under the supervision of Dr. Mengele, conducted regular selections. We saw scores of women being marched off. We didn't know if these women were selected to go to work camp or what their fate would be. The empty barracks were soon filled with new arrivals, women who still looked like normal people in spite of their baldness, well fed, and their eyes not yet apathetic.

A few days after our trip to the showers, we had to move to another barrack.

"Schnell! Schnell! Sofort! Sofort!"

The new barrack was 150 metres closer to the entrance of the camp; the rest was the same. As we had no belongings, the move was fast and effortless, the reason for the move unknown and quite unimportant. The routine was the same as before. Every few days somebody from our group spoke to someone who claimed to know about some of our men. I was a bit skeptical of all the stories. Our men were supposedly on the other side of the crematoriums in Auschwitz, but I couldn't comprehend the enormous dimensions of the place. What we had seen appeared to cover many kilometres, and that was apparently only a small part of the Auschwitz-Birkenau complex.

I stayed together with my friends in the new barrack, and we got to know each other better. Lucy and Netty Slager each had three children, all of them in hiding somewhere in the Netherlands. Netty had three daughters and Lucy one daughter and two sons. The husbands of both had come with them in our transport. Lenie was married but didn't have children. Then there were the young girls like Margot and Anne Frank, Annie Levy, Teta Cohen, Bloeme Emden and many more.

One morning we were marched outside the camp, this time to work in the Mexico Lager which was close to BAIIB. When we arrived, we saw many men at work. Besides the SS guards and the Jews, there were political prisoners. We could recognize them because they wore different-coloured outfits from those of the Jewish men. A third colour was worn by the common criminals who were in Auschwitz instead of in jail. Several Capos were also present, Jewish prisoners who worked for and with the Nazis. They were hard, tough men. I was afraid of them, and I stayed out of their way.

Our job was to carry sand, and I looked forward to a chance to talk to the men. Maybe somebody knew Bernd or Hans or something about the war. We were told to carry the sand to the right-hand side of the road, even though the camp wasn't built up there.

We arrived with the sand, and in front of us was an enormous pit with hundreds or maybe thousands of dead men, women and children, piled one on top of the other.

33

The hole had to be filled. I never spoke to anybody.

After only a few days in the second barrack, we were moved again, after a selection by the doctors, this time across the Lager Strasse. The day we moved, Tuesday, 26 September, was Kol Nidre, the night of Yom Kippur, the most sacred evening of the Jewish year and the beginning of a day of fasting. Lucy and I had decided that in spite of everything we were going to fast.

We ate our ration of bread as if it were a home-cooked meal. I remembered that at home my mother always had soup and chicken with rice. As I child I never liked rice, but in my mother's home you ate what was cooked. The exception was the meal before Kol Nidre. Then my mother would have a big dish of boiled potatoes, just for me. I could almost taste them that night.

Besides the Dutch girls, there were mostly Polish and Hungarian women in this barrack; we hadn't a chance to meet any of them yet.

As soon as the sun had set, a spontaneous outburst of prayers started from all corners of the barrack. Some were praying in their native tongues, some were chanting the Kol Nidre in Hebrew with loud, clear voices, some were weeping heartbreakingly, some were standing still, praying within themselves and some were just lying on their bunks.

The outpouring of emotion stirred up many thoughts in me. We didn't blame the Almighty for our terrible lot. Our belief had not been rocked by the Germans. Maybe that was a part of what Judaism is all about.

The next day, Yom Kippur, was of course a working day as usual, though the bricks or the grass we had to move felt a bit heavier than on other days. At soup time the ones who were fasting didn't claim their ration. It was impossible to keep it hidden and save it. Maybe the other people got more. At night when the time came for the bread to be passed out, the guards asked those who had fasted to step aside. If you were honest and stepped aside, you missed your ration of bread. We did. They outsmarted us again.

By now the fall had come, and with it cooler and wetter weather. Our thin dresses could hardly protect us from the hours standing and working in the windy autumn weather. Chasing us up and down the Lager Strasse was still one of the favourite games of the Nazis. Another was sending us to our bunks, and as soon as we were in our bunks screaming at us "Extra Zahl Appel. Schnell! Schnell!" You had better be fast because the whips were flying through the barrack. All we had to do was put our shoes on. My poor shoes. I seldom had enough time to open the laces or put them on properly. I just put my feet into the shoes any way possible and ran.

We kept trying hard not to lose our sense of humour. Some days it seemed to be almost impossible. We all had our bad days, but we tried, if any of our friends had a low day, to help her over it with optimism and hope. I don't know which pain was the worst, the constant worry and sorrow about one's family, the never-ending hunger pains, the fatigue or the humiliation. I felt as if somebody had cut my whole stomach open and was using a sharp garden rake on my intestines, which had become raw and bare.

The rumours were a constant thing in Birkenau as the weeks started to count up toward the five or six that I believed the war would last. Sometimes a little doubt began to creep into my mind, but I discarded it.

In the meantime, I'd become quite accomplished at sneaking up in lines. I'd found out that the closer one was to the end of the soup line, the smaller one's portion became. However, I never tried to go twice for soup. I had seen too many women try to go again only to be whipped almost to death by some Nazi.

The selections by the Nazi doctors became more frequent. We didn't know what the gentlemen had in mind, and the rumours were never far when a selection started. Lucy and I tried to go toward the end of the line, hoping the Nazis might stop before they came to us. Indeed once or twice the selection stopped before we were looked over.

As the middle of October was almost upon us, a terrible new fright took hold of me when I started to realize that my brother's prediction was not going to come true. The Germans seemed to be still in full control of everything and everybody. It took a lot of talking from my friends to keep me going. I decided I had to come back in case any of my family should make it. I felt it was harder for a parent to lose a daughter than for a daughter to lose a parent, and I was convinced that Bernd would make it, though I never again set a date for the end of the war.

Thirst was still with me. In the evenings when I went to wash up a bit, I always had a few sips of the water, sometimes wondering why I hadn't become sick from it. Maybe the precautionary measures my parents had taken in 1942 of having all of us vaccinated against typhoid, cholera and so on kept me from catching anything.

We went for another trip to the showers. This time the smoke was coming out of the chimneys while we were standing almost in front of the crematoriums. It was beyond my comprehension. I was in a trance.

Within a week, we were moved from one barrack to another several times. Every move was preceded by long hours of counting, recounting and selection by the Nazi doctors. All other activities had come virtually to a stand-still, and it seemed that even the rumours had gone on leave.

Every day hundreds of women were selected from the BAIIB camp and marched away.

On the morning of 26 October, we were still in the barracks when the orders came. We were to take off our clothing, and to hold the clothes in one hand while stand-ing next to the bunk. In spite of the countless selections, the women from our transport were still left together.

After a while Dr. Mengele and another young doctor entered the barrack, and we had to walk slowly past them, one by one. The Nazis looked me over, made some remarks, to which I didn't listen, and told me to walk straight out of the barrack. Outside, I put on my clothes and looked around for my friends. Nobody spoke a word, but all our eyes were searching for the faces that had become so familiar and dear. I didn't see Netty, who had been walking right behind me. Nor did I see Anne or Margot Frank, Mrs. Frank or Mrs. van Pelz.

We stood for hours on the same spot. Many other women from the barracks next to ours and across the camp road joined us as we stood and waited for the Nazis' next move.

Several hours had passed when I heard a familiar voice whispering "Move over. Make room for a friend."

It was Netty. I held her hand. No questions were asked, and somehow Lucy, Bloeme and I moved her in beside us.

It was five years later that I found the courage to ask what had happened to her that day, and perhaps only then was she ready to tell me.

When Netty's turn had come to walk by the doctors, the Nazis commanded her to go to the right and not, like many of her friends including me, in the direction of the exit. She was pushed toward the entrance of a small room. Orders were yelled to deposit all the clothing one was holding in a container and proceed into the room. Inside the room were naked women like sardines in a can, scared to death, some crying, some praying. More women were being shoved into the room all the time.

After the first terrible shock, Netty realized she was still holding onto her clothing, and her brain started to work overtime. She had to get out of this death-trap and rejoin her friends, but how?

Then she discovered that on the opposite side of the room there was another door. The next several hours Netty spent desperately trying to inch herself forward in the direction of the door while holding onto the clothes.

Finally she reached the door, opened it and found herself standing outside. She slipped her clothes on and walked away. She was almost overcome with excitement when she saw us still standing in front of the barracks.

None of the women who were in the room survived the war. Anne and Margot Frank, Mrs. van Pelz and others went to Bergen-Belsen. Mrs. Frank apparently remained in Birkenau and died during the winter.

Those of us who'd been sent outside stood more or less the rest of the day in the same place until we were absolutely exhausted. My mouth and tongue were sore and swollen. I assumed it was from drinking the polluted water.

Late in the day all the women who had been waiting on the camp road were assembled. We had to go on a long march, in rows of five, of course, outside the BAIIB campsite into BAI camp on the opposite side of the railroad. I was too tired to be much concerned with what would happen next. We stood outside all night, next to the showers and the crematorium. I slept part of the night standing up. Somehow the morning came, and I realized we were standing Appel and we were being counted. And counted again.

Then we were ordered into a large room with tiers of benches which reminded me of my biology room in high school. I sat on the first bench, glad to be able to sit down, and noticed everybody was climbing up the back of the room.

"Aren't you afraid down there?"

"No. What's going to happen is going to happen. I can't do anything about it."

Some SS women with heavy boots, whips and guns came in and told us how lucky we were to be chosen to work for the Fuhrer. I didn't believe a word they were saying. The next order was to take off our clothes and go through a door into a great shower-room which we had never been in before.

Was it a shower-room or a gas chamber? The only difference was a drain on the shower-room floor. Thank the Lord, this room had a drain.

Again we went through a draughty hallway into a large hall, which looked almost like a bazaar with stands against the walls. The stands were piled high with clothing that had been confiscated from people as they entered the camp. One side of the hall had only underwear, one side shoes and stockings; another side had dresses and coats to please even the most discriminating shopper.

We were going to be outfitted for the winter because we were going to leave Birkenau to work in factories in Germany.

It wasn't quite like going to a store and choosing something appropriate for the occasion. My first stop was for underwear. Each stand had several SS women handing out clothes. I received one pair of underpants and one undershirt, both of tricot material. I put them on and went to the next stop, where I became the owner of a dark-blue dress with white polka dots. It wasn't my choice, but at least it fitted, and most of the dresses looked too small for me. The pair of socks that were handed to me turned out to be fancy cotton knee-socks, one beige and the other a pinkish colour. Not too good for a long winter. Now on to the shoe department.

"What size?"

"38."

I was hoping for a warm pair of shoes. The SS woman had all kinds, small and large, open and closed. I tried on a pair that didn't fit me at all. The woman gave me one look, took a pair of fancy shoes with four-centimetre heels and hit me hard a number of times over my bald head.

"Here, you swine," she screamed, "have some shoes for the winter. They'll keep your feet dancing in the snow."

The shoes were at least a size too small, but there was nothing I could do.

The last stop was for a coat. Here I was luckier than with the shoes. I got a warm black coat with a big collar and nice wide sleeves. The one piece of clothing that wasn't obtainable at this bazaar was a brassière.

We had very little time to admire each other's winter fashions. As soon as everybody had acquired their clothing, we had to assemble outside the building to be counted. The next order was to march to the station.

Would I really be leaving this hell on earth?

We were all loaded into the freight cars of a very long train. The car was empty except for a large drum for toilet use. Each of us received one slice of bread, one empty can without a label and one spoon. This was our baggage. We were leaving Birkenau with all its pain and sorrow, but we had no idea what was in store for us next.

In spite of my sore mouth and 30 hours without sleep, I felt a little hopeful. While we waited for the other cars to fill up with the women of the work transport, they came around and put something in our cans to drink. One of the guards saw that I couldn't eat my slice of bread because my mouth was too swollen, and after I suggested to him that I might be able to smoke one of his cigarettes, he gave me one. It tasted very good after months without.

I don't remember much of the trip. I slept most of the time, as it was dark inside day and night. Most of my companions were discussing what was going to happen to us, but all I wanted to do was sleep. The train stopped several times. Sometimes the guards let us empty the drum at these stops. At other times we could feel that parts of the train were taken off. As we learned later, these cars proceeded to different work camps. Through the cracks in the walls, we could see that the landscape was changing, but we couldn't see much else.

About the middle of the next day, we arrived at our destination, a place called Libau in Silesia. The cars were opened, and we found ourselves looking at a little empty country railroad station. It was a dull fall day. We were exhausted, hungry and thirsty after lying in the freight car all during the long trip. It felt good to stand up again. My mouth and tongue seemed to be more swollen than before.

Looking around, I saw a big mountain like a picture postcard. Unbelievable what seeing something green did to me. In Birkenau nothing was growing, no trees, nothing at all. It always seemed to me that the Germans tried to destroy not only the human beings but everything that was living and growing in this world. Somehow they couldn't destroy our determination to live.

"Oh how beautiful it must be here in the spring," I exclaimed.

"How can anybody be so naive and optimistic as to even think about the spring," my friends said.

It wasn't always easy, but I kept on trying.

The train was emptied; 300 women came out. From our original Dutch transport there were about 45 of us left. The rest of the women came mainly from Hungary, some from Poland and a few from Belgium.

We were assembled on the platform and, after being counted time and time again, we marched for a while until we found ourselves standing in front of a large building. We went inside through a main entrance and then upstairs to a sort of cafeteria with long picnic tables.

Some of the women SS guards spoke to us. All this looked a little unusual to me. I knew you couldn't trust them for a minute. Our meal, which consisted of potatoes and cream cheese, looked very appetizing, and there was plenty of it. We hadn't had a meal in days so everybody had a feast . . . but I couldn't eat because of my mouth.

The Lager Alteste, a very charming Hungarian Jewish woman, was one of the 200 prisoners who had arrived in Libau before us. She was a go-between for the prisoners and the SS guards. She came to me to find out if I was sick.

"Oh no, not sick, just a little swollen mouth. But I

would appreciate lots to drink."

She brought me a carafe full of some surrogate broth which we came to know very well over the next several months.

On the way out of the cafeteria I saw myself in a mirror for the first time. I couldn't comprehend that this long skinny face and bald head were mine. Everybody had a turn looking into the mirror. A lot of teasing went on about entering a beauty contest. We couldn't decide if big ears would be an asset or a hindrance.

Soon afterward we found out, to nobody's surprise, that our first meal was the one and only time we were in the cafeteria, and it was also the only time there was enough food available.

But we were still alive, and we had left behind us the most devastating, inhuman place on earth. No more showers, no more gas ovens, no more smoking chimneys and no more smell of human bodies burning.

7

The first night we spent in a big building that was used as the administration building and the living quarters of the German guards, both the men and women.

At the head of the camp was the commandant. If we were to address him, which never happened, we had to call him Herr Kommando-Fuhrer. He was a tall middle-aged man with a bored expression. We never found out just what role he played, but I think he had an extremely lazy life with lots of women and fun.

There was the head of the female guards, whom we had to address as Frau Kommando-Fuhrerin. She seemed to be running the show. Then there were the female guards, some young, some older, but all of them ready at any time to scream, swear and hit. They had to be addressed as Frau Aufseherin. If we addressed them, we had to be very polite and courteous. Their vocabulary was overflowing with swear-words and other unpleasant expressions.

The 200 Hungarian women who had already been at Libau for some time had lived in this big building. These women had built the camp and done some very heavy work, digging the hole for the latrine, putting up the barracks and moving and assembling the bunks.

Our first working day started with an hour of Appel at five AM, after which we were divided up into several groups. One group was to give the camp its finishing touches, another had to unload a freight train near the camp. I was one of the latter group. I still felt very tired, and my mouth was about the same as the day before.

The freight consisted of raw materials for the three factories that were located in Libau and also some supplies for the camp. We had to unload the materials and carry them in very large baskets.

The unloading was closely supervised, the guards checking and rechecking the freight. The baskets, which were carried by two people, seemed to become heavier and heavier as the day went on and my strength became less and less. I carried on till well into the afternoon, when one of the guards saw me fall under the weight of a basket and wanted to know why I was slacking off. After she saw my mouth, she sent me, accompanied by another guard, to the sick-room in the building where we'd slept the night before. The doctor was a Polish woman, a prisoner of war but not Jewish. She was a woman of medium build with a round face, high cheekbones and nice blond hair, probably never shaved. She examined me, but didn't say much. She let me gargle and have a sleep.

As we soon came to know, the only two drugs available in the camp were Noritt, a charcoal-black tablet, and Permangan, a red tablet. Noritt was originally used for settling a hangover. In Libau it was used for everything from a fever to any possible internal ills. The Permangan was an antiseptic tablet and was used whenever Noritt wasn't. If it didn't help you, by the same token it didn't hurt you.

So it wasn't hard to play doctor here. We often doubted if the Polish woman was a doctor at all, but it really made no difference.

I fell asleep immediately and woke up some hours later when I heard them say that food had arrived. I felt somewhat better. Sleeping in a bunk instead of in a freight train or on the floor had given me renewed energy. I was able to eat some soup which tasted very good to me. Later, when we had it six days a week, it was something else. I announced to the doctor that I felt completely better. I'd only been a little tired. She wasn't convinced but said that maybe it would be wiser to join the others.

I was escorted to our new living quarters, Stube 7. I'd arrived none too early; the bunks were being assigned only to those who were present. Most of my friends were in Stubeb 7, and they were loudly proclaiming that I was coming back and they must keep a bunk for me. When I entered, cheers went up. I stood confused, not understanding what was going on.

Each of us got a bunk to ourselves here. The bunks were narrow wooden beds with thin straw mattresses and a grey cotton blanket. My bunk was in the far corner, on the bottom, with dear Lucy in the bunk above me. I was pleased by the thought of not having to feel the bodies of other women against me all night.

Stube 7 was the smallest room in the camp and had only about two dozen bunks, which were stacked two-high along the walls. The only other things in the room were a big round stove, a pail to be used for washing ourselves, and a pail and mop to keep the Stube clean. Keeping the barracks and the grounds of the camp clean was an obsession of the Germans, and we were going to spend many hours at it.

Outside the door of each room was a barrel to be used as a toilet during the night. The Germans found it easier to keep an eye on us that way rather than having everybody running to the latrine. I was glad of any reason not to go to the terrible latrine as it was impossible to use it normally.

From the outside the latrine looked the same as the barracks, only smaller. Inside, it was just a sand floor with a long narrow plank running the whole length of the barrack. Under the plank was a deep hole. When I sat on the plank, not only was I afraid of falling into the hole, but it was somehow built on an angle so one wet oneself every time. It didn't take me more than a couple of days until I'd mastered the trick of urinating forward in a standing position. As for a bowel movement, I made use of the big barrel at night, just as most of us did.

The barrel of course got full, and it always seemed to be at that point that I had to make use of it. Then, under the guards' searching eyes, one had to cart the barrel to the latrine and empty it. It was nobody's favourite job, especially in the cold, snowy winter nights. Once in a while somebody would fall in the snow with the barrel. The next day some lucky crew would have to clean it up, and all the prisoners have a couple of hours Straf-Appel, which meant a couple of hours standing outside in any kind of weather. This also meant a couple of hours less sleep.

Our days in Libau started at 4.30 AM, when an Aufse-herin accompanied by a big German shepherd banged on the door and screamed at the top of her voice "Aufstehen Zahl-Appel." A few well chosen swear-words were added to finish the morning greeting.

The morning Appel was usually an hour long. After the Appel on the second day in Libau, all the Dutch girls were marched to the factory. The Nordland plant was in a very large building. They manufactured snow chains for all kinds of military vehicles, from small to very large. To supply the German army for the winter in Russia took a great many chains. On the way to the plant my feet were hurting me because my beautiful party shoes were much too small. I could already feel big holes in my fashionable knee-socks, and the winter hadn't even started.

When we arrived at Nordland, we were divided into several groups. The foreman, an old German civilian, explained something about the production of the chains that we were all very excited to learn.

"Wer kann schweissen?" he said. Who can weld?

I knew that *schweissen* in German is *lassen* in Dutch so I said I could. I was soon to master the trade and so did many other women.

Since I was supposed to know how to weld, I was put in charge of the rejected chains. A couple of the girls who worked with me turned out to be just as experienced as I was. We had to inspect the whole chain and re-weld the weak spots, and we had to keep up a certain rate of production.

One of my co-workers was an interesting young Polish

woman who knew for certain that her whole family had been killed. I couldn't let myself think that about mine. She hoped to be able to go to Israel and start a new life after the war, but she wasn't too optimistic about surviving that long.

Five non-Jewish men, university students, three from the Netherlands and two from France, worked in the foundry and as general mechanics. They were what the Germans called Studenten-Arbeitseinsatz. They were not in Germany voluntarily; they'd been forced to work in the German factories to replace the men who were fighting the war or plaguing the Jews. The boys lived in limited freedom. They had an apartment and a radio, and they could do what they wanted except they couldn't leave Libau. When the Dutch boys found out that some of the women came from Holland, they were delighted. We were absolutely forbidden to talk to any of them; we could only talk to each other. The Aufseherin kept a close eye on us, but we often managed to exchange a few words when one of them came to do maintenance work on the machines. To talk to free people from the outside world, even a couple of sentences, seemed unreal. The boys weren't able to do much for us, but to know they were there was a real moral support.

Once in a while when I had to deliver some rejected chains to the other parts of the plant, I got an opportunity to exchange a few words with them. My shoes didn't fit any better than the day they were assigned to me. They were deteriorating fast, my feet were hurting and the winter was almost upon us. Whispering, I told the boys about my shoes. I don't know what I expected from my pleading, but I was, as so often, desperate.

One morning a few days later, when I took my position behind the machine, I felt something on the floor. I looked down and saw a pair of men's shoes. They were far from new, but to me they appeared the most beautiful shoes in the world and a priceless gift. I never found out who put them there.

After the first three or four days in Libau, my mouth was better, but my eyesight had weakened fast, probably due to a vitamin deficiency. My work output was down. At work I often closed my eyes and had a little nap. One day the foreman caught me dozing, and all hell broke loose.

"Don't you like your welding job? Are you too lazy to do your duty? I had better inform the Kommando-Fuhrerin about you right away so she can take the appropriate measures."

"I'm not too lazy. I love welding, but I can't see my work well enough. Because in Auschwitz the SS took my glasses from me."

This last part was true, but I was like the illiterate farmer who went to the eye doctor for glasses so he'd be able to read. I couldn't have seen any more with my glasses, but I told the foreman that if I had glasses I could perform my job much better. He said he would look into it. In the meantime all I wanted was to be able to see my bread and food.

Lucy helped me as always through those hard days.

About two weeks later I was on the way to the washroom to fill up a pail of water when the Kommando-Fuhrerin called out to me.

"Hey you there." People didn't have names in the camp. "Aren't you the one who needed glasses?"

"Yes, Frau Kommando-Fuhrerin."

"I just received word that you can go to Camp Grosz Rosen and get a pair of glasses tomorrow."

"Frau Kommando-Fuhrerin, my eyes are so much better I don't need the glasses any more."

That was fine with her; it saved her a lot of work and trouble. And maybe it saved my life. What I certainly didn't need was to go someplace without my friends and with a chance to see some more gas ovens. My eyes were improving and pretty soon were back to normal.

This Kommando-Fuhrerin was a small woman about 35 who looked more like a kindergarten teacher than the commander of a concentration camp. Soon after my meeting with her, and to nobody's surprise, she was replaced by two real SS women who were going to take care of things. We had an extra Appel, and they introduced themselves. The new Kommando-Fuhrerin was a woman about 30, of medium height, with a face that suited her job perfectly and a harsh voice. She had a whip in her hand at all times, and we soon discovered that she loved to use it. Her assistant was a different type. She was a fat woman with a pretty face, and she was accompanied by a big German shepherd whom nobody trusted. In her hand she also had a whip. She was a woman of many moods; sometimes she'd want to talk to one of us, almost as one human being to another, and other times she was cruel and savage. She was a lesbian and had for her private use a little room next to Stube 7. From my bed one could see through the planks that formed the wall, especially when our lights were out and the lights in the little room were on. She had plenty of choice in lovers, but thank goodness she didn't want me or any of my friends.

Another person who had to be regularly supplied with lovers was the Kommando-Fuhrer. When he was ready for a new body in bed, we were called out to an additional Zahl-Appel, and he would walk from one row to the next, looking up and down, assessing each of us. I had a special facial expression for occasions like this. I'd practised looking imbecile, and I never faced the person who was inspecting me. I can't imagine what he was looking for. Every one of us was a pitiful sight, undernourished, in rags and with little or no hair.

Those women who were chosen by the Kommando-Fuhrer were never seen back in the camp again.

8

In Libau, we had Appel twice a day from 4.45 AM till 5.45 AM and for an hour or longer in the evening after everybody had finished eating. And on Sundays for endless hours. We stood in rows of five, and the distance between each person had to be just right. The original purpose was to count bodies to make sure nobody had disappeared, but that could have been done in a couple of minutes. The time spent on Appel, I found, was the time when I was most alone. It was the time of greatest fatigue and hunger, and it was always terribly cold. I would put the collar of my coat up as far as possible over my neck and head. The sleeves of the coat were wide, so I put my left hand inside my right sleeve up to the upper arm and the same with my right hand on the left side. My legs were bare and so was my head. Somehow the middle of my body would be the coldest part of all. Many thoughts went through my mind in those cold dark hours. I had certain patterns to keep my memory alive. I said to myself the addresses of all my relatives overseas, in Canada, the USA and Brazil, like a directory, so that after the war I could somehow get in touch with them. After the war . . . it seemed like a joke.

All the good advice I'd received from my parents came back time and again. My father had told us about the pogroms and the massive killings of Jews over the centuries and how there were always survivors. The surviors, he would say, have a duty to carry on. Maybe I was going to be a survivor, if only the pain in my stomach and the cold in my bones would ease for a moment. Sometimes I'd look around me and see a young woman in a nice warm coat and hat with something on her legs, and I'd be envious of her, but then I'd realize that she would be just as cold in about five minutes. My mother had taught me early in life the foolishness of envy.

I had one story that came back to me regularly in Libau. In my first year of high school, I'd been taught the Greek and Roman myths. When I heard the story about a young lad who'd been asked at the beginning of his life to make a choice—did he want an easy life first and later a hard one, or did he prefer a hard life first and later an easy one?—I had said to myself in school, I wish life was like that and somebody would ask me. I knew what to answer, first hard and then easy. Standing there in the cold, this fable puzzled me; maybe I was being asked. Maybe from now on things would get better. They could hardly get worse.

If I closed my eyes for a moment, a big glass of warm chocolate milk and a piece of buttered bread would pop up. Such dreams never lasted too long before an Aufseherin would have something to scream about or some job that had to be done.

One bright frosty Sunday afternoon, we had been standing for several hours when I was one of the ones chosen to fill the baskets with coal for the stoves. The coal was buried under a huge pile of frozen snow. We had to dig it out with our bare hands, which was a rotten job. We had eight stuben and the guard-house to supply with coal that day which meant nine baskets. My hands were like icicles and my body was rigid when the Aufseherin asked me how many baskets had been filled.

"Nine baskets, Frau Aufseherin," I replied, politely, but without counting them.

She counted the baskets, and there were only eight. She gave me a good slap. My face was stiff from cold, and her finger marks stayed indented in my cheek. After filling the ninth basket, I went back to our warm barrack to find some relief for my frozen body near the stove. My friends would find some way to lift my spirits with a sarcastic joke.

We worked six days a week in the Nordland factory, and it seemed like five too many. Nordland paid the SS a set amount a day for each prisoner the Nazis provided to work for them. Renting out your slaves, you could call it.

The first part of our working day in the factory was from 6.30 AM till noon. Then we marched back to the camp under heavy guard. In the dining-room we ate our soup. After lunch we assembled and were counted, and we all marched back to the plant. The afternoon working hours were from 1 PM to 7 PM. At night, after we returned from work, we had our supper, which was soup again.

Our menus didn't have much variety. At noon the soup usually had something swimming in it, but never meat. About four days a week it was made of some sort of dried vegetables. We called that Straw Mattress Soup. Other days it had traces of potatoes, but it was never enough. The pain of hunger was constantly with me, the last thing at night before I fell asleep, in the middle of the night, first thing in the morning—always the same ache. Our evening soup, besides being a smaller portion than the noon one, was often just boiled water with a bit of flour to thicken it and maybe, in the first three months, some salt. After three months, all our food was without salt.

Following our evening meal, we had an Appel of at least an hour. Afterward we received our daily bread ration, a small piece of a round brown loaf. The size of our portion varied. When we were first in Libau, our ration was a quarter of the loaf a day, but that didn't last too long. Soon it was down to a sixth of the loaf, which was equal to only one thick slice. A couple of times a week we got some butter, about the size of a finger, other days maybe a slice of cheese. I didn't always eat the butter; some days when the skin of my face or my hands was extremely dry and rough, I'd use it for my skin. Sometimes Lucy and I would use one ration of butter for external and one for internal consumption.

It took the greatest self-control not to bite into the bread and finish it right then and there. The next meal was the soup at noon the following day. I learned to save part of my bread for the morning as my breakfast. At set times, we got containers of liquid for the whole stube. It was a solution of some kind of tree-leaf boiled in water, and it tasted all right.

Sundays we got only one meal. Some time during the day we'd have our soup. Our bread ration was smaller too. On Saturday night we'd receive bread for two days, but instead of receiving two portions of a sixth of a loaf, we got only one sixth and one eighth. It doesn't sound like a great difference, but for a person suffering agonies of hunger it was.

One Sunday, for some unknown reason, our meal was hot vanilla custard instead of soup. The sweetness of the custard tasted ever so good, but my stomach couldn't handle it, and I became sick. Another Sunday, the Nazis who were in charge of the kitchen surprised us with some pieces of crisp fried bacon instead of soup. I had never eaten bacon in my life, as my parents kept a kosher kitchen.

"What are we going to do now?" I asked Lucy, who was as wise as a rabbi.

"There is absolutely no problem," she explained. "The Jewish laws were made for the people not the people for the law, and we need every piece of food we can get our hands on to survive. Not only are we going to eat it, we are going to say special blessings and enjoy it."

And so we did.

♬

For several months, Nordland was so busy supplying the army on the eastern front with badly-needed snow-chains for their tanks and heavy trucks that the decision was made to have the plant operate on a 24-hour basis. From that day on I was transferred to the big welding machine. No more light-weight chains for me, only the huge ones for tanks and trucks. Soon I became an expert at welding snow-chains. I also learned to be very careful, as we had no gloves or masks. After a few burns I found ways to prevent too many more. I began to know the chains for the tanks best; their weight was tremendous. They arrived on a trolley, and three of us had to lift the heavy lot to the table. All the larger rings had to be welded. That meant we had to lift the whole lot every time a ring was done. The smaller rings on the chains had already been done on smaller machines. Some of these jobs were done sitting down, something we were envious of.

We had final control over what happened on our table,

and that gave us a chance to slip an unwelded ring through once in a while. We hoped somebody would get stuck in a Russian snowbank.

Another kind of sabotage was possible because of the shifts. The Aufseherin changed shifts too, so before each shift change we were to count the finished chains that lay on a second trolley at the end of the table, ready to be wheeled into the foundry where the Dutch and French boys took care of the final process. We always managed, even under the watchful eyes of the Aufseherin, to count a few more than were on the trolley. Because the next shift had to fill the trolley up to a hundred chains, the Germans would never know who counted wrong. It was too heavy for the Aufseherin to recount the whole trolley once it was loaded.

Sometimes the management thought an order was filled and ready for shipment and at the last moment they found the order was five or ten short. Everybody ran around angry, screaming, swearing, unable to find out where the mistake had been made.

That was the only good thing about the night shift. It seemed to take just about everything out of me. As we didn't return to camp till morning, we had a break from midnight to 12.30. The break was murder. We got some of our tea, and we could eat our bread if we had any left, but often I was too tired even to do that. After ten minutes of the break, the light was turned out for the rest of the half-hour. I always fell asleep immediately, either on the floor or leaning against something. When the lights came back on, I had a terrible time waking up and would be nauseated from fatigue.

One night I looked up from my work just in time to see something flying through the air. I put my hands up and caught a pair of unfinished knitted wool socks. They had no toes and no heels, but I could wear them as socks since my knee-socks were no more, or I could wear them as a sort of gloves over my hands. I was very happy with my new piece of clothing.

When we arrived back at the camp in the morning, after a full night's work, we had our morning count. Then the ACF usually had all kinds of chores lined up for us. The benches and floors in the dining-room had to be scrubbed. Sometimes when we were finished with the job and hoping to get some sleep, the Aufseherin would take a pail of water and throw it on the floor so we could clean it up again. Then the washroom had to be scrubbed. We might be sent to bed and no sooner get to sleep than the day-shift came into the camp for lunch. The girls would be popping into the stube to warm up a bit at the stove. Awake again. Often we were glad they came in because in the daytime somebody might hear news from the war. The war was at a sort of standstill in October 1944, and even in November. One day we heard that the Americans had just re-elected President Roosevelt for a fourth term. I could hardly believe it. It had never happened in the USA before, and I thought maybe somebody had made the story up. The next day we found out; it was the truth.

After the day shift had left for work and we had fallen back to sleep, there would be a loud banging on the wall.

"Mittagessen ihr verschlafene Schweine."

Dinnertime, you sleeping pigs. Up again, half-asleep, dragging our feet to the dining-room, telling each other that this was a midnight supper. We are going dining with attractive, elegant men. What a hard time we'll have choosing from the extensive menu. May we suggest something, Madame? Our chef's specialty for the day is a delectable soup.

How could we resist?

We didn't have to wait in line because only those on night shift were eating now. After lunch more jobs had to be done. One of my least favourite jobs was cleaning the latrine, but it didn't matter; we did everything with pleasure. Other afternoons were spent unloading freight trains. That was always a difficult job.

Often on Sundays in the winter we'd move a pile of snow from the left side of the camp to the right side. The purpose of this chore was to give another crew of women the opportunity to move the same snow back again. No shovels or other tools were used for this exercise, only our bare hands and large baskets.

In the factory we alternated shifts each week but worked with the same girls all the time. After a while we were changed around again, this time to my great advantage. I got an easier job and began working with my dear friend Bloeme.

Bloeme and I were to sit and sort rings which were spread out on a large table and had to be put into small cartons. What an easy job! It gave us a chance to talk and get to know each other better. Our conversations had a certain pattern every night. First we told each other about our families, then about our fears and worries and finally our favourite subject: what do you imagine liberation will be like?

Bloeme told me all about her parents and the loving home in Amsterdam she and her younger sister had grown up in. Her parents and sister had been arrested and sent to a concentration camp quite some time before Bloeme, and she was afraid they were dead.

We recalled our high-school days. Bloeme had graduated from high school at an early age, but it wasn't her intelligence that stood out for me, but her warm friendship and her sense of humour. We tried hard to see something funny in almost any situation we found ourselves in. I told Bloeme about my parents, my brother Bernd and cousin Hans.

Hans was the oldest son of my father's youngest sister, Lotte. She and her husband, Leo Badmann, had lived in Amsterdam. When my parents found out that Hans' parents and younger brother Ernst had been arrested and sent to a concentration camp but that Hans was still free, they asked Jef van Bebber to get in touch with him. Jef went to Amsterdam and made all the arrangements for Hans to join us in our hiding-place.

The van Bebber family's willingness to help and to share all they had with us and several other Jewish families is beyond words. Mr. and Mrs. van Bebber, Agnes, their youngest daughter, and their son Jef, who was in charge of the whole operation, dedicated 24 hours a day to us. They were heroes.

One afternoon, shortly after Jef got in touch with him, Hans stood in front of us. He and Bernd began to share the 39-inch mattress on the floor of our front room while I slept on a folding bed. In the daytime my bed and the mattress would be stored in a corner so we had room to sit around the table we used to eat on, to play bridge with the other hiders in the house and of course for my parents' daily ritual of double solitaire, the winner receiving 25 cents. My mother always got very excited if she won, and soon the whole house would know about it. She was always in a good humour. Bernd and Hans also had their daily card games, with side bets on the length of the war, what would be for supper, or what the weather would be the next day. Anything to keep oneself occupied.

We read a great deal. Downstairs in the middle of the day, we'd listen to the Free French newscast on the radio, and at six o'clock we'd listen to the BBC news from England, always hoping to hear of advances by the Allied troops and always second guessing all the generals' decisions. Wednesday night was our concert night. When the Allied airplanes flew over on their way to bomb Germany, sometimes for hours we heard nothing but zum-zum-zum, a wonderful sound since it meant the Allies hadn't forgotten us.

We were never afraid of what was going on in the air, but we were never without fear of any noise or cars in the street. When the front doorbell rang, we disappeared into the washroom, behind a door or into a closet. We'd remain there until the coast was clear again.

The van Bebber family and all those hiding in the house would spend the evening together downstairs. Mr. and Mrs. van Bebber had several married children living in Tilburg who'd come and visit, but except for my girlfriend Doortje Evertse, they didn't encourage anybody to visit their house, afraid the neighbours would notice something unusual. It took a great deal of care to pretend that in a house where sometimes as many as twelve people were hiding, there was only a family of four. Mr. van Bebber spent most of his days shopping. At any given place, he only shopped for four people. Jef would buy food stamps when any were available from one of his many connections in the underground organizations. Some days Mr. van Bebber would be busy all day riding his bicycle into the country trying to buy vegetables and fruit for all of us. He was a baker before his retirement, and on special occasions we'd be treated to one of his original creations. On Passover he surprised my father, who was going to give a Seder without matzos, with some flat, round, delicious buns, a good imitation of matzos that we really appreciated. Mrs. van Bebber did all the cooking, and Agnes took care of many of the extra errands as Jef had an office job and was gone all day. One of her errands was taking the train to Leiden every ten days or so. Her brother Jan and his wife Lenie were the cooks for the Orts-Kommandantur of Leiden. As it became harder and harder to buy food, Jan and Lenie kept the kitchen of the van Bebber household supplied. Agnes would travel to Leiden with a couple of large empty suitcases; they were stuffed to capacity on the way back with meat, shortening, sugar and flour. Agnes, like Jan and Lenie, took great risks in these operations.

It was very important that between 4 and 6 o'clock in the afternoon no lights be turned on upstairs so as not to arouse any suspicion about extra people in the house. This is how our daily "round-table" meetings began. My parents, Bernd, Hans and myself would sit around our table, and each afternoon somebody would have to speak. We talked about everything, about a book we were reading or had read, about the past, the present or the future. My father liked to recall his years as a young man when he lived in Brussels. He was the oldest son. He had four sisters and a brother. They had been a very close-knit family, and my Dad had wonderful stories about each one. We got to know the whole family very well indeed. He remembered every possible date, every anniversary, each cousin or nephew's birthday. One day he said, "Today my sister Hilde and her husband have been married 25 years, so let us rejoice and be happy for them."

He talked frankly about his experiences in life. He was a religious man in a conservative way and also a great realist who had read a great deal and tried to pass his optimism and *savoir vivre* on to us. Neither he nor my mother would refuse to discuss any subject with us. We were free to ask about any topic in the world and a lively debate was certain to follow, sometimes to be taken up the next day where we left off.

My mother had read a great deal too. Her favourites were history or historical novels and autobiographies. She liked to recall the athletic accomplishments of her youth. She had been a good swimmer and tennis player and had several crystal vases and other mementoes of tennis matches she'd won, and she was very proud of them. She'd been an accountant in her father's bank during and after World War I and had many amusing anecdotes about that time in her life. She and my father had met while she was working in the bank. She had an unbelievable recall of phrases and catchwords in several languages and never missed an opportunity to use them.

Opposite the van Bebber house was a butcher shop, and on Wednesday afternoon the meat for the week would be delivered. We all sat behind the curtains watching this great event.

"Good business prospects," my mother would say.

My mother knew Hans and I were good friends who could, if we were able to find a private spot, talk for hours about anything young people talk about. She kept her eyes open to make sure it was only talking.

Once during the winter of 1943-44, Bernd became very ill and a doctor had to be brought in. The doctors in Tilburg would respond in emergency cases and come at night to see a person in hiding. Bernd had to have complete bed rest, so he was moved in with my father, and my mother took my bed. Hans and I were on the mattress on the floor. My mother gave us full instructions. Each on his own side, don't move toward the middle, keep under your own blanket. I don't think she slept a wink.

"Hans, you are getting too close to the middle."

"Anita, move back somewhat."

The end result was that Hans and I slept on the floor with the mattress between us, and my mother was tired out in the morning.

When it was Bernd's turn to speak out at the afternoon round table, we learned more about his high-school and college days. His final high-school exams were written under war conditions in May and June 1940. His high school was occupied by the German army so they had no more classes after 8 May. The final exams for all the high schools in the country had to be written on a given date. He wrote his finals in the attic of the Technical College. Bernd attended one year of college; then he was forced to leave school like all the other Jews. He had many non-Jewish friends who were majoring in business and economics. They supplied him with an enormous amount of study material, which lasted well through his time in hiding. My father and Bernd would often study together, and my Dad was always proud of how fast Bernd could master a new subject.

When Hans had his turn to talk, he told us what had happened to his family. The Germans invaded the Netherlands on 8 May, 1940. Like so many other people, the Badmann family wanted to flee before the Germans could occupy the whole country.

They lived in Amsterdam and had heard through friends that at the Prinsengracht in central Amsterdam, people were gathering and taking buses from there to Ymuiden, the North Sea harbour closest to Amsterdam, and from there going by boat to England.

They went downtown to the Prinsengracht and made the arrangements to leave the country. The buses were standing in front of the building, and except for Hans and his father, who had stepped inside the building to make some last-minute inquiries, the whole family went into one of the waiting buses. The bus was filling up quickly, and my aunt began to wonder what was keeping her husband so long. She decided to have a look, and her son Ernst left with her. No sooner had they gone into the building than the buses left with grandmother Badmann and Hans' fourteen-year-old sister, Irene, neither having any identification or money with them. The four Badmanns came out and saw the buses had left, but everybody assured them more buses were coming. They waited and waited. They tried to get a taxi. They returned the next day, but all their efforts were in vain.

Then came the long months of uncertainty and waiting. What had happened to them?

Almost a year passed before the Badmanns received word from my aunt and uncle in the United States that Irene was in England and that, after an ordeal of several months, she had made contact with a second cousin of her mother's in Manchester. The grandmother had fallen downstairs while in a prison in England and broken her hip. The combination of this fall, her age, the heartache about everything that had happened to her and Irene and the worries about the rest of her family hastened her death, which occurred soon afterward.

Hans was a handsome, tall young man who had done well in high school. After his graduation, he'd worked as a carpenter, but he was looking forward to continuing his studies after the war. He often talked about his hope of becoming an engineer. He wanted to build highways and bridges all over the world.

When it was my turn, I talked about how disappointed I was, one day during my summer vacation from school in 1941, when the caretaker from the high school came to our house to let my parents and me know that I and all the other Jewish children were no longer allowed to attend classes. It was a hard job for the caretaker to bring this kind of message, but it was war, and we were living under the German occupation.

Then there was a very boring time. My non-Jewish friends went back to school; my Jewish friends and I helped our mothers. We weren't allowed to do any kind of work outside the home. Bernd could no longer attend college. Soon some Jewish people got together and organized a workshop for the young men like Bernd and the older men who had lost their jobs. The workshop was located in the large storage area of a factory. Several trades were taught, including carpentry and upholstery.

The Jewish teachers had also lost their jobs, so it was only a question of time before a Jewish high school was established for the southern part of the country. After many difficulties, the school opened in the spring of 1942 in s'Hertogenbosch. It meant daily commuting by train, which turned out to be lots of fun, even though we had to wear a big yellow Star of David. The Dutch people were never unkind to us because we wore a star. We could only sit down after everybody else in the train was seated, but we didn't care about that. The school was located in an old uninhabited building with plenty of empty rooms. Our teachers were a combination of university and high-school teachers, plus an engineer who taught us chemistry. We had very good teachers.

It was a rotten time to be a teenager because we could not go anywhere for entertainment, but we had a marvellous time in school with the new friends we made from other cities. All this didn't last very long. The school year ended in June, and nobody knew what would happen to any of us in the next few months. The summer of 1942 was a hard time for the Jews in the Netherlands;

many thousands of them were arrested and sent to concentration camps. Our family was lucky. The Nazis hadn't come for us yet.

When the school opened again in the fall, many of the students and teachers had been taken away. Replacements for the staff had to be found, not an easy task. My mother was very reluctant to let me go back to school. First of all, it had become more dangerous to travel by train wearing a star, as the Germans occasionally arrested people at the railroad station. Also, my mother needed my help in the house. She wasn't allowed to have help any more, and we had a large house.

After long discussions with both the principal and the teachers, and after promising to keep up my studies, I went to school three days a week, and the rest of the week I helped my mother at home.

Every night in Libau, as we sorted out metal rings, Bloeme and I would tell each other these things. Then we'd turn again to our favourite subject: what would liberation be like? Bloeme would start to dream out loud.

"It will be," she told me night after night with only small changes in her words, "a beautiful spring day. The air will be soft and mellow, full of promises. The birds will be singing a song of love and rebirth, the trees will have started to get their new leaves. Maybe some spring flowers will be blooming in the gardens, and our hearts will be happy again."

"The first thing when I get home," I said, "will be to take a long hot bath, wash myself with nice-smelling soap, dry myself with a soft towel, brush my teeth with toothpaste, comb my hair and get dressed in clean clothes. Then I'll sit down at a nicely set table, with a table-cloth of course, and china plates, and enjoy a home-cooked meal."

At this point we'd pause to put together a menu that would satisfy any gourmet.

"Then I'll go to sleep in a real bed with clean sheets and just lie there and be thankful."

The mirage vanished quickly with the appearance of one of the Aufseherinen, who hit me over the top of my hairless head with a long iron bar to make sure I didn't fall asleep before the shift was over.

The thought of what home would be like wasn't allowed to interfere with the daydreams we told each other every night. But even as we dreamed and hoped, the reality that we had no place in this world to call our home was with us.

10

One day during December, the Nazis decided that Stube 7 would be transformed into a sick-bay. The Dutch girls were all to join the other Dutch women in Stube 8. The other few inhabitants of Stube 7 would join their own countrywomen.

The move next door didn't take any time at all. Stube 8 was a much larger room than Stube 7, but it had to accommodate a greater number of women. Lucy and I and the rest of my friends were lodged on the right-hand side of the room.

One of our young women, Floortje, was elected or appointed Stubenalteste. It gave her no privileges, only duties. She was the one to tell us when it was our turn to wash the floor or clean the barrel, to fetch the carafe with our morning drink or look after the fire in the stove. We also had a system so that once a week everybody in the room had a turn for a warm wash. We'd go and fetch the pail of ice-cold water from the washroom, bring the pail back into our room and warm the whole thing on the stove.

When it was my turn, I'd first wash myself (without soap or a towel of course) from top to toe and then wash my underwear in the water. Then I dried myself and the clothing near the stove. I always hoped no unexpected Appel would come before I was dry.

Some nights I'd go to sleep as early as possible and not bother with anything or anybody. Other nights I'd talk to my friends, wondering why they chose me as their friend, or I'd watch the other women trying to encourage each other. To live together with so many women from so many different backgrounds was an experience of great importance for me. Time after time I'd realize how essential our comradeship was in the fight to survive.

Over the winter, several of the women combined their talents to come up with a medley of songs about our life and our hopes. We added new words to some well known melodies. On Saturday nights, as we sat on our beds, a few girls would start singing and soon everybody would join in.

One day about the end of January, we were working the day shift, a little bit more fed-up and a little bit hungrier than usual. Rumours were flying about the advance of the Allied forces, but as always nobody knew what was the truth and what was just wishful thinking.

The office at the Nordland plant was about eight steps above the ground, so the management had a good view of the whole operation. We hadn't talked about it, we hadn't even thought about it, but just as we were ready to go back to the camp, about 30 women stormed up the stairs to the office and complained about the long hours we had to work. We were hungry, tired and fed-up, we told them, and with the poor food we were getting, we weren't able to perform the way they expected. The manager of the plant, whom we nicknamemd Blondie, was employed by Nordland and not by the SS. He spoke to us and told us there was nothing he could do. And we'd better know who was the boss, for they hadn't lost the war yet.

Within a few moments the guards were there, and we were thrown back down the stairs. I was pulled down the edges of the stone stairs on my back. I got up slowly and in pain.

We had to assemble to march back to the camp. The guards were furious, hitting out left, right and centre. Nobody could escape them.

"Does your back hurt, Anita?" Lucy said to me half-way back to camp.

I couldn't look at her. I was afraid I might start to cry.

"Don't you ever ask me anything like that again," I said.

The road back to camp seemed much longer that night because of my sore back, but in spite of this I was feeling great because of one word.

Blondie had said the Germans had not lost *yet*. Maybe we could outlast them.

Slowly I was getting to know most of the women in our new stube. Some talked about their children in hiding, others about children who'd been arrested before them. I knew whose husband had been on the same transport as we were and who'd already lost loved ones. We were all a terribly heartsick bunch.

One of the young women, Donna, was in her early thirties. Her bunk was near mine, and she too told me her life story. She was a prostitute. I was nineteen years old and still green; I'd read about prostitutes but certainly never met one. She went into great detail about her life. She had an apartment in the Hague where she entertained men and made them happy, she said. Occasionally she'd have a steady boyfriend. She also had an eight-year-old girl who was safe, she hoped, hiding somewhere in Holland. Never, Donna said, did she deal with any German men, civilian or in uniform. She would never lower herself to them.

Donna wasn't what I'd call a good looking young woman, though she did have a nice figure. In the evening before we went to sleep, she'd often turn and twist her body a bit and tell me all she wanted was a good man in her bed. She had no patience with lesbians, she said. She could wait till she was back in the Netherlands for a real man. Donna was in fact a loner who apparently didn't need the close female friendships most of us had.

One day word came that Dr. Mengele planned to honour us with an inspection visit. We all knew only too well what an inspection from Dr. Mengele meant, and I was really scared. What did he have in mind this time?

The Aufseherinen were absolutely hysterical, screaming and running around yelling "Sauber! Sauber!" The floor had to be scrubbed twice and the bunks had to be just so. The blankets had to be straight on the beds, and we had to stand in a certain way next to our bunks. Don't talk, don't move and don't breathe. Donna noticed that I was extremely tense and upset.

"Anita, don't be afraid," she said. "I'll take care of Dr. Mengele for you and all the girls in the stube."

At last Dr. Mengele arrived with the Kommando-Fuhrerin and the commandant. This was one of the few times the commandant took part in the action. Mengele took a look around the stube, and Donna somehow caught up his attention with her eyes while the Kommando-

Fuhrerin was talking. He kept on looking at Donna and never noticed anything or anybody else in the stube. After a few moments that felt like hours, the Nazis left. We never found out the reason for the visit.

One of the young girls from our transport I'd got to know in Birkenau was Teta Cohen. She was with several woman from Leiden, the Hague and Rotterdam. When we arrived in Libau, Teta found herself the only one left from her group, and she became part of our circle of friends.

Teta was in her early twenties and came from Leiden. She loved to talk about her family and her expectations of life after the war. In the late fall, she started to cough, and we soon realized that she didn't have a normal cold, but we never let her know of our suspicions. For a long while she worked alongside us in the Nordland plant and never missed a day of work.

One day toward the end of January, the management of Nordland decided we should have some special privileges, some paper to be used at the one toilet in the plant. The toilet itself was a fantastic luxury. Nordland was looking for a person to take care of the paper and keep the toilet clean. It was an easy job and through great luck we got it for Teta. Working was becoming harder and harder for her. She had started coughing more frequently and was spitting blood.

Somebody had dug up some old city directories for the year 1921-22. Teta's job was to tear up the books for us. Each page was torn into small pieces, and she would hand out one piece at a time. She also had to keep the toilet clean and tidy. As always in life, it's important who you know; Teta supplied me with extra paper. Instead of just one piece, she'd give me three or four. After a little while I was able to build up a nice reserve which kept me going for some time. I hid my little treasures in my bunk and felt very rich.

Teta fought till the very end. One day near the end of February, she could no longer stand for Appel. We had to take her to the doctor. Since she was beyond Permangan and Noritt, they sent her to the sickroom in the big building, the same room where I'd spent an afternoon when we first came to Libau. Just once four of us were able to visit her there. There were four other sick women in the room. Teta hadn't given up hope and was still talking about coming back to our barracks. The sick didn't receive any nursing care. They were left on their own except for a guard watching over them. A few days after our visit, we were told that Teta had died.

One of the three plants in Libau manufactured caskets, and this plant supplied the caskets for anybody who died in the camp. They always delivered two caskets at a time. One was used, and the extra one was placed in the washroom. First thing every morning we could see it there.

The Germans didn't know what to do with our dead, so they let us bury them outside the cemetery in Libau. It was at the opposite end of the town from the factories. On our daily trips to and from Nordland, we were far away from the populated area, and the people of the town didn't see much of us. The only people who came into contact with us were the few civilian women who worked in the factories.

To bury Teta, we had to carry the casket through the town to the cemetery; all the town people would see us from close up. The guards wanted to show everybody in town how well they treated their Jews and how well we were all dressed. The seven of us who were going to bury Teta were fitted out with clothes that belonged to everybody else. I got a pair of shoes from somebody whose shoes looked almost like new, a coat, hat and gloves from somebody else. By the time we were ready to go, we looked almost like normal women, but every coat had a square cut out of it in the middle of the back. In its place was sewn a piece of different-coloured material. If one of us tried to escape, she could be spotted immediately.

It was one of those beautiful warm mornings when the sun is trying to melt the snow. Having gone through all the cold weather with hardly any clothes, the heavy clothing we now had made us unbelievably hot. All the way through town people came out of their homes to have a good look at us.

Two Aufseherinen accompanied us and kept a close eye on us. Just after we finished digging the hole, one of them said to me, "Did you come along to see where you'll be buried?"

"No Madame, I won't give you that pleasure," I said. "I came to pay my last respects to a friend."

Thus risking another slap in the face.

We buried Teta and said farewell to her. Lucy said the prayers and a few words. Teta was one of the very few who had a last resting-place and was buried with human dignity.

11

Night shift was something that belonged to the past. Nordland wasn't busy any more. As the weather got better, the snow started to melt. The snow-chain season was over.

Our ration of bread became smaller about the middle of February. The salt supply in the kitchen must have run out because the already tasteless soups were now without salt. Rumour had it that the Allies had bombed a large food depot near Breslau and belt tightening was in order. Our belts could hardly get any tighter. We were terribly hungry. One day Lucy and I were doing some chores behind the kitchen barracks when we found a large garbage-pail of potato peels. We hid as many as we could in our coats, careful not to get caught. Back in the stube, we roasted the peels against the stove. While we were waiting for our feast, we reminded ourselves that the best nourishment of the potatoes is in the skin.

It was February when our room became infested with cockroaches and wood lice. First a few, but within weeks they'd multiplied. At night they crept out of the wooden walls to feed on the wood of the bunks. They also attached themselves to human beings. Several of the girls had open sores on their legs and arms. Somehow the round terrible things didn't like me. They'd walk over me but didn't bite. But how I hated them!

By the middle of March, the snow had all melted, but the weather was still wet. As usual we were very hungry. We could hardly talk about anything except food. All during the winter, we had talked about food and recipes. Now this conversation never stopped.

"Judith, repeat your recipe for the angel-food cake so we can memorize it."

Judith would answer, giving the amounts of sugar, butter, flour. And six eggs.

"Did you hear that? Did everybody hear that? Judith makes her angel-food cake with six eggs. How can anybody make an angel-food cake with only six eggs?"

"My angel-food cake has at least seven eggs, sometimes eight or more."

From angel-food cake, we went on to butter cake, a Dutch favourite. Should we make it with a pound of but-

74

ter or a half-pound? Should we use almonds or not? What kind of almonds would we use? What does your chicken for Friday-night dinner usually weigh? Only four pounds! What kind of stingy person are you? My chicken is always at least five pounds, and then we have soup, fish and many other good things.

The same conversations went on, over and over again. Exchanging recipes, putting together elaborate menus for holidays, all while nauseated from hunger.

About this time, in the early spring, I worked with ten or twelve other girls unloading turnips from the freight trains. We had to load the turnips into large baskets and carry them past the guardhouse into the camp kitchen. Even after six months of turnip soup, they still looked good. We took turns hiding a couple in our coats. That went on for some time without rousing the suspicions of the Aufseherinen, until one day the girl who was walking ahead of me tripped and two turnips dropped out of her coat right in front of the Aufseherin's feet. It was a comic sight, but it meant the end of the turnips for us. All of us were searched then and there. I had to open my coat and out fell my two turnips.

One morning toward the end of March, a large number of the women who had been working in the factory were ordered to walk in the opposite direction instead. We walked about half a mile up the road, and then we had to climb the beautiful mountain with its tall handsome trees. All through the winter I had looked at the mountain. Sometimes it was covered with snow, sometimes not, but I always got a good feeling just looking up at it.

There were no roads or paths on the mountain; the ground was moist from the melted snow and slippery from old leaves, and the roots of the trees were sticking out, making it very hard to walk. We climbed the mountain and went on up some other hills. After a long hard climb, we arrived at large plateau where a number of men were waiting for us. I was absolutely exhausted from the trip, but the day had only started.

We were to build an airport on this rugged terrain. The tools to build the runways were shovels and our hands. The men we had to work for were miserable rotten brutes who thought these undernourished skeletons of women could work as hard as they did.

Some of the women had to go to a quarry, where for days they were blasting with dynamite. The Germans intended to build a secret hiding-place for their airplanes in the quarry. Lucy and I were outside on the plateau, turning earth, sorting stones, being sworn and screamed at. At the end of the day, we had to walk back down the mountain to the camp, another long, tiring trip.

We worked six days a week on the airport. The work was the same every day, very heavy. One day Lucy and I were working as usual when one of the men gave Lucy a hard blow over the head and knocked her down. He was screaming and swearing at her. All of a sudden I was so outrageously angry, I lifted my arm and was going to swing at the maniac when Lenie came from nowhere and gently drew my arm down.

"You don't want to do that Anita," she said.

"Oh yes?" I said. "Do you know what that man did to Lucy?"

"Yes, yes," she said. She went on talking to me for a long time to calm me down.

Another day when four of us were digging stones out of a narrow ditch with our bare hands, my patience was tested again. The stones had to be loaded into a cart, which was pulled by a horse. The German labourer who came with the horse took an instant dislike to me. He harassed and pestered me all day. I paid as little attention to him as possible, which seemed to provoke him even more. Finally he ordered the horse, which was standing above me, to kick me, knock me down and finish me off. I couldn't move, so I started to talk to the horse in a very low voice. I told the horse, in Dutch of course, that he was a nice animal, and I knew he wouldn't hurt me. I just kept talking and talking. Whatever threat the German made, the horse stubbornly stood his ground.

The weather was very important to us, as we were outside all day, unprotected from rain, wind or sun. Sometimes it rained all day, and we were soaked to the skin. After a rainy day, the mountain was very slippery, and I used to fall or slide on the way up and the way down. The plateau must have been far away from the populated area because we didn't see a single house or farm in the hills, nor did we see any people except the ones we worked for and the guards.

I used to watch the clouds very closely to figure out how long it would be before the sun came out to warm us up. I played a game with the clouds. In high school I had a geography teacher, Mr. de Groot, who made us draw all the countries of the world as well as the bigger islands so we'd always be able to recognize them. Now each cloud would be an island or a country, and I tried to think of which one it was. When I looked next time, the clouds had moved, the pattern had changed, and I had to start again with a new mystery map.

In the evenings, as soon as we got back to the camp, we talked to the girls who were still working for Nordland. They were our only link with the boys and the news about the war. Would we still have a chance to see it end? Our strength was diminishing fast. Something else had complicated my life terribly, the invasion of my body by lice. These parasites take on the colour of the garments you're wearing, and one can't see them, only feel the constant itching. At night we'd take our clothes off, and by holding the seams of the dresses and our underwear against the stove we tried to get rid of the lice. We never quite made it.

All during the winter, I'd tried to keep my hands tucked into the sleeves of the opposite arm to keep them warm while we stood for Appel. My hands always suffered a lot from jobs like moving snow and digging coal, but I never worried about it. Now, working on the airport in rain, hail and wet snow, with heavy winds, they became swollen and very sore. At night I'd look at my hands and wonder if something should be done. But what? Going to the doctor was the last thing on my mind. She had never really helped anybody.

One weekend in April, my fingers turned dark. The next morning right after Appel, I went to the Assistant Kommando-Fuhrerin and asked her very politely if I could go and have Frau-Doktor look at my hands. She had a temper tantrum. I was too lazy to work, and I wasn't going to see Frau-Doktor. The only thing that would cure my hands was working in the fresh air.

So I went to work, but to my great surprise that night she came looking for me and ordered me to go to see the doctor. Frau-Doktor told me that I had frozen fingers and after the morning Appel, I must come to the sickbay for treatment.

The next day was the first of May. After everybody had left for work I stood for a moment outside in the spring air, alone, no Aufseherin, no fellow prisoners, just me and the world. I went to see the doctor, and she decided that warm compresses of Permangan and rest would do the trick.

In the sick room were about twelve other women with various ills, which were all being treated with one of the two wonder drugs. Some women were resting on the bunks while others were talking quietly in Hungarian. My understanding of the language was limited to a few words. As soon as I got the compresses on my hands, I went to sleep on one of the bunks. What a luxury to sleep in the middle of the morning.

Shortly before lunchtime I got the compresses changed and then I went to join my friends, who were still working in one of the factories and had come back for lunch.

They had amazing news. Hitler had committed suicide. He was dead! Yes, it was true, it was really true. The boys had said it over and over again. Yes, you may believe it, you can believe it, you must believe it.

I wasn't able to at first. But I went back to the sickbay and called out "Girls, Adolf Hitler has committed suicide, he is dead. That is the truth."

To me the Hungarian women weren't like the Dutch girls, who had laughed, composed songs, helped each other through the terrible ordeal. I knew very little about these women except their outcry *"Mit gsinaljak?"* What should I do?

All that changed that very moment. The sick, fragile, famished women lifted me off the ground, put me on their shoulders and carried me round and round the room, singing and praising the Lord. When somebody put me down, a couple of others would come and pick me up for another round.

"Why carry me around?" I said. "After all, I didn't kill Hitler.

Oh they knew that, but I had been like the angel who brought the good tidings from the Lord.

The pleasure of being able to bring good tidings was a new experience for me. All afternoon, while nursing my hands in more Permangan baths, I listened to happy and excited voices. I was looking forward to sharing the news of Hitler's death with my roommates who were working at the airport.

Again and again doubt crept into my thoughts. What if it wasn't true? Would I be able to cope with another disappointment? Finally the afternoon came to an end, and I could tell my friends the fantastic news. They were very happy but also surprised that no German, neither civilian nor guard, had behaved differently from any other day.

Our happiness brought a whole new set of questions into the foreground. Would the war come to an end? Would the Nazis let us live? Who would I see first, my mother, my father, Bernd or Hans? I could almost feel them embracing me.

Reality came back with our evening Appel, which seemed to last forever. Afterward it was business as usual. Some women had their turn to wash themselves and their clothes, others had their turn cleaning the floor. But the air was filled with anticipation, and it took many hours before the women in our room were able to calm down and sleep.

The next morning, 2 May, started as all the other days had at 4.30 AM. Nothing had changed. My hands felt a bit better, and I wanted to be with my friends. After Appel and a drink, we went back up the mountain.

We were eagerly watching for any kind of change in the Germans' behaviour, but if they knew more or were scared, they did a great job of hiding it from us.

The day dragged on and on; we couldn't wait to get back to the camp to find out what was new. Our disappointment was great when we found out that nothing had happened since the death of Hitler. The boys said they would keep us posted and advised us to carry on.

Never, during all the months I'd been a prisoner had I experienced the anxiety I was feeling now. The next two days were marked with rain, sun and wind. Friday night, 4 May, after we'd returned to our room from the evening Appel, we were called back out for an extra one. What did the Germans want from us now? Were they going to shoot us all?

Those who'd worked on the airport had to step forward and make rows of five. I was in the first row. The Lager-Fuhrerin, who had very seldom concerned herself with us in the past, had taken charge of the Appel. She informed us that all the women who had worked on the airport that day would receive an extra ration of bread. We couldn't believe our ears. That wasn't all; we'd also receive shoes. She gave us a story about how hard she had tried to get shoes for her women. She asked me what size of shoes I wore. I told her the size, and she threw a pair of open wooden shoes toward me. As I bent over to pick them up, she looked at me and howled "What is the matter with your hands? They're black."

I looked down at my hands. It was as if I saw them for the first time.

"Oh that," I said. "They're frozen, Frau Lager-Fuhrerin."

"Frau-Doktor, Frau-Doktor. Come here right away and see."

The doctor came.

"Have a look at these hands. What's the matter?"

"Oh," the doctor said. "She has frozen hands."

"What can you do for her?" the Lager-Fuhrerin wanted to know.

"Well we can bathe the hands, and then let them rest."

"Okay, this one will never work again."

I couldn't believe my ears. I was allowed to keep my shoes, since there was hardly anything left of my old ones, but since I wouldn't be working the next day, I didn't get the extra piece of bread. I felt great envy for those who got the bread. Probably they were envious of me because I didn't have to work any more.

The fifth of May was a cloudy day. I'd promised my roommates that before I went to the sickroom to bathe my hands I'd clean and wash the floor and get water ready for washing when they got home. I felt almost like a big shot walking through the camp in the middle of the day.

It started to rain, and the rain became heavier by the hour. In the middle of the afternoon, all the women who had worked at the airport came back to the camp. They'd heard the civilians saying to the Aufseherinen "Are you trying to drown them here? If you're wise, you'll take them back to the camp." They were absolutely soaked, and the little clothing they had on looked as if they had stood under the shower for hours. Everybody took their clothes off, and we tried to dry them.

Notwithstanding the wet clothing, everybody had to stand Appel as always.

"Monday morning you're going back to the mountain," the girls were told.

Sunday the sixth of May started like any other Sunday in Libau. Then shortly before noon, somebody heard a loud voice outside the camp. Two of our women immediately went out to the washroom with a pail. Outside, they saw two of the Dutch boys walking on the road beside the fence. They weren't allowed to talk to us so they shouted to each other.

"Did you hear the good news, the Netherlands has been liberated, the Netherlands is free. Please keep calm, please keep on going, please be careful."

When the two women came back with the news about the liberation of Holland, the tension in our room became almost unbearable. The anxiety and anticipation was beyond description. We even started to argue with our friends, something that had seldom happened before.

Sunday night passed, and Monday morning arrived with Appel at the normal time. The women who had been working in the factories were going to stay in camp for the day, but just for today, they were told. All kinds of jobs were waiting for them. The women who were working on the airport left at the usual time.

After I'd cleaned our room and helped scrub some latrine pails, I was going back to the sickroom to nurse my hands. Around the time I finished my chores, the women who were supposed to work at the airport returned to the camp. The civilian workers hadn't shown up, and without them our women couldn't work. The Aufseherinen told the women that the civilians didn't show up because it was too wet, but that tomorrow they'd return. Everybody was kept extremely busy all day, but nothing really happened except more rain and mud.

That night must have been one of the longest nights ever. The tension in our room had grown even worse. The next morning, my roommates chose me to go out and investigate since I was the one who officially didn't have to work any more. I went out to the latrine to see what was going on. It was around 4.30 AM.

I didn't notice anything out of the ordinary. It seemed time to be awakened, but nobody came to call us, so everybody stayed in bed.

A little later we heard a commotion outside. Where

the hell were Die Höllander? The door of our room was pushed open, and the assistant Lager-Fuhrerin stood in the door with her big dog in one hand and a whip in the other.

"Who do you think you are, not to come to Appel? I'll teach you dirty pigs. You'll stand an extra hour of Appel tonight. Now fast, fast. Hurry, you lazy dogs."

We were outside in no time, taking our places. First we got a long lecture about our disobedience. We were going to pay for it. We stood even longer than usual. Finally the Kommando-Fuhrerin came and inspected us row by row. Then she spoke to us, as if we were human beings, in a normal voice.

"Go," she said. "Get something to drink, make your beds, clean your rooms, and then go back to bed and rest."

Had we heard right? Were they going to poison us or shoot us? As always, we did what we were told. We were very suspicious about the next move the Nazis would make.

After we had finished cleaning up the room, I was sent out with a carafe to go to the kitchen for more drinks, but mostly to see if anything new had developed. The clock in the guard-house said ten to eight. All the Aufseherinen were gathered together, apparently in a great discussion. I went back and reported my findings to my friends, who tried to outguess the Germans. I just went to sleep.

"Wake up, wake up. Don't sleep your life away. The war is over. The Germans are gone. They've run away into the mountains."

A dream.

"No, no, it isn't a dream. It's true, the war's over. The Nazis are all gone."

I opened my eyes.

"We're alive, and it's the first sunny day in May," said Bloeme.

12

The war is over. The war is over.

I went outside, not even trying to comprehend what it meant that the war was over and we were free women. I walked slowly around in the most glorious sunshine the world had ever seen. Looking at the other skinny girls and women in their rags, I realized for the first time that most of us had reached about the end of our physical strength. We looked like the skeletons we had seen in Birkenau.

Nobody had yet left the camp grounds when the five students who worked at the factory arrived at the gate. They had found a horse and had stolen and slaughtered it, and they were going to take care of us all. They carried the meat into the camp kitchen and promised us a good meal. They advised us to stay in or near the camp. Our guards had fled, with their weapons, into the mountains, and nothing was clear yet. They wanted to make sure that nothing more would happen to any of us.

We sat in the sunshine, relaxing and daydreaming and waiting for our meal to be cooked for us. The soup, with its generous supply of soft-boiled horsemeat was like a feast: no chef could improve on it. Second and third helpings were readily available. No bickering, no pestering, no screaming, no swearing. Peaceful and thankful.

A few of us went for a stroll toward the town, but I kept looking over my shoulder expecting any moment that an Aufseherin would yell at me. Nothing like that happened, and we walked along the same road we had walked countless times on the way to the factory. I saw trees and landscapes I'd never noticed before. We didn't stay out too long as we had no idea what would happen next. We were in no-man's land.

The next morning was again a glorious day. The students were busy in the kitchen, but we were ready to start taking matters in our own hands. During the morning came word that the Russians were on their way, and they'd like us to be there for a celebration. Several hours later two truckloads of Russian soldiers arrived. One very tall soldier came forward and asked us nicely in Yiddish if we would all come and join him and the other soldiers in commemorating the victory over the Nazis.

Everybody came and stood around, not in rows of five, but just the way one wanted, standing or sitting on the ground. Several soldiers stood on tables and took turns delivering speeches in Russian to celebrate the great triumph. The tall soldier was the last one to speak. He spoke in Yiddish, with great passion and devotion, trying hard to get us in the right mood for the occasion. To our surprise, he succeeded. We finally felt it. We were free!

Soon he had us singing the International. Then we were singing all the national anthems of the countries we came from. We ended with a very emotional singing of Israel's anthem, Hatikvah.

The Russians asked us what they could do for us. We told them food, food, food, and some clothing. They promised us everything and all the help we needed.

The next day we heard that some women had been raped when they went for a walk into the town that night. So much for Russian help.

It was time to investigate the world and start finding out for ourselves what to do with our lives. We walked to the town. Except for the day we buried Teta Cohen, we had never seen anything of Libau.

But it wasn't what I saw of Libau that made an impression on me. It was the hundreds of refugees travelling with horse and cart or on foot, singly or in whole families. These people, all of them displaced by the Germans, were on their way back to their homelands. All they had with them was what they plundered on the way. We saw them entering homes, going on a rampage, opening cupboards, taking whatever took their fancy, leaving the places an absolute shambles. Of course the Germans had done the same thing all across Europe. Were people ever going to be decent to each other again?

In Libau we found where we could obtain bread, a whole loaf. A whole loaf for one person. We only had to order it in the bakery, and we could pick it up the next day.

Although we were free, we had to get used to being able to walk around on our own. I wasn't self-conscious about my rags, but the German people gladly gave us some clothing. They were happy enough if only we didn't ravage their houses. We'd walk along a street, look at a door. Maybe we might each get a pair of underpants? Sometimes we were lucky and got what we asked for. Most of all we were interested in obtaining food. Our hunger hadn't let up at all. While exploring Libau, we found ourselves at the railroad station. Not very interesting, but toward the end of the little station we noticed a few small storage buildings. Some other women from our camp were coming out, smiling happily. We looked inside, and there in front of our eyes were countless sacks of sugar. No time to waste now. I lay down on my stomach on top of a sack, tore the thing open and used both my hands to shovel the sugar into my mouth. The pleasure was enormous. After our sugar feast, we discovered more interesting surprises stored away, scores of cardboard cartons filled with brand-new flannel floor-wipers which looked to me like the perfect material for a skirt. I took several of the cloths and felt extremely happy at the thought of being able to wear something new. Soon I could discard my blue polka-dot dress forever.

Back at the camp, we investigated the cafeteria of one of the factories and found it well stocked with dishes and cutlery. I helped myself to a heavy white mug. A possession. Something of my own. I still have it; my husband uses it every year as his Passover cup.

Behind the factory, a field of new potatoes was looking at us, and soon we were digging them up and bringing the potatoes to the camp kitchen.

At the camp, things became more difficult daily. Our toilet facilities had always been terrible. Now that we were all eating as much as we could find, everybody had diarrhea. The possibility of an outbreak of sickness was great. It was time to make plans to leave. Many of the Hungarian women had already left the camp and started back to their homeland.

The five students had let it be known that they would each take responsibility for one person on the way back to the west. Their choices were five of our closest circle of friends. That left Lucy, Netty and me.

Lucy had worked at Nordland with several German civilian women. One of them had always said to Lucy that if she could ever help her she would. Now was the time. Lucy got in touch with the woman and explained to her that the hygiene at the camp was at a point where we wanted to leave immediately and that we only needed shelter for a short time as we were in the process of leaving Libau. The following day Lucy got the answer; two could stay at her place and one with a friend of hers who had a farm close by. We had to decide who would go to the woman's house and who would go to the farm.

Netty and Lucy felt I shouldn't go to the farm alone. Netty would go to the farm, and Lucy and I would stay together. We said goodbye and good luck to our friends and promised again to contact their friends and relatives in the Netherlands as soon as we got back. We walked out of the camp, a week after liberation, into the great unknown. I felt newborn, but with the difference that when a baby enters the world, it doesn't have to make decisions. It slowly grows into the way things are. I was grown up, nineteen years old, in a place called Libau. I didn't even know where to find it on a map.

We found the place where the woman lived. It was a big stone apartment house, surrounded by a number of others just the same. Her apartment, like all the others in the building, was very modest, consisting of a large bedroom and a kitchen. In the bedroom were twin beds, several cupboards, some chairs and a couch. Lucy shared the bedroom with the woman and her eight-year-old son. I slept in the kitchen on a cot. The hall outside the apartment had a tap and sink for the use of all the apartments on the floor. Downstairs near the back entrance were toilets for the use of the tenants of the building.

The woman's husband, like those of most of the other women in the tenement, was somewhere in the army. As a hostess, she was helpful and nice, and very proud of her little apartment. We really didn't need anything but shelter. We were gone practically all day, gathering food and getting ready for our trip home.

The other people in the building were anxious to catch a glimpse of Lucy and me. We noticed doors being left open just enough to peek out. It amused us, but we had no time or desire to talk to anybody except to obtain information we needed. We learned that to be able to travel, we had to acquire papers from the Russians. They didn't have a commissar in Libau. The closest one was Grussau about ten kilometres away. We had no time to lose. Early the next morning, Netty arrived with enough food for a couple of days, and the two of us set off to get some papers. Lucy stayed in Libau. She and our hostess were going to do some sewing. Out of the floor cloths they sewed a skirt for me and a good-sized carrying-bag for each of us. That way we could transport our food and anything else we wanted to carry with us.

Netty and I started to walk; as always, we talked a lot. Netty was extremely anxious to get back to her three daughters and was still hoping her husband might come back too. After a while we were getting tired and thought of hitch-hiking. A car was coming, and a little hesitantly we put our hands out. Nothing happened; the man looked us over and drove on. After all we weren't a good-looking pair. The traffic on that road was light, and it was some time later before a truck came in sight. No longer reluctant, we stood in the middle of the road with our hands up. The Russian army truck stopped, and a soldier started to talk to us. In Russian! Somehow we made him understand that we wanted a ride with him to the next village. When he signalled that we should sit with him in the cab, we showed him that we wanted to sit in the open truck.

Well shaken up, we arrived in the village, a very small place, and had no trouble in finding the Russians. They were in a sort of office building with a waiting-room that had benches all around the walls. We entered, and a Russian soldier approached us and asked us in German what we wanted. I answered and told him that we wanted to see the commissar and that we needed papers and advice for our trip back to the Netherlands. He asked us to wait for a while. Nothing happened, and we became very hungry. We informed the soldier we'd be back after we'd lunched in the village. Lunch in the village was finding a park bench and eating our bread and cheese.

We went back to the Russians and waited and waited. We became impatient, and I asked the Russian soldier what was taking them so long. He went to see the big man upstairs. A few minutes later he was back. The commissar wanted me to come upstairs, but not Netty.

"We both go upstairs or nobody is going upstairs," I told him. We wanted the papers, but if they didn't want to give them to us right here, we didn't want them at all. We'd been pushed around long enough by the Germans. I wasn't ready to be pushed around by the Russians now.

The soldier went upstairs and was soon back down again. This time he wanted all kinds of information from us. Which way did we want to travel? We had no idea which way to take so we asked him which would be the best. He couldn't tell us. There were several places where fighting was still going on.

We decided we were going by way of Czechoslovakia. After more waiting, the man came back with a piece of paper which he handed to us, saying "This is exactly what you need. Have a good trip." The paper was all in Russian, and it had a sort of seal on it. We thanked him and set out on our journey back. This time we wasted none of our energy, but put out our hands right away and got a truck to take us all the way to Libau.

Now that we had our papers and knew which direction we wanted to go, all that was left to do was to get enough food together to last the three of us for several days. That meant a lot of bread, for our appetite hadn't decreased yet. Every day we ordered as much bread as the baker would allow us. By the end of the week we'd have what we felt we needed to travel with. The baker probably thought that if he gave us as much as possible, he could get rid of us.

Our hostess told us where the shoemaker was, and we went to visit him. We had the wooden shoes we'd got a couple of days before the end of the war and we asked the shoemaker to reinforce them so they'd last for the whole trip back. He had only wood and artificial leather to work with, but he did a good job.

The farmer who sheltered Netty was very kind to her. He gave her a small wheelbarrow which we were to use to carry our food and a few belongings. The wheelbarrow was a funny sight, but it was our first tangible possession and gave me great pleasure. It was a present from a human being, one we had received without begging or stealing.

Another thing Netty got from the farmer, which turned out to be of no less importance, was an address and a personal letter to a friend of his in the town of Trutnow. Trutnow was the first town we'd pass through on our trip to Prague, and his friend was the town butcher.

13

We left Libau on 19 May, shortly before 5 AM. The wheelbarrow was loaded to the brim with bread and other food. In our bags we had our little bit of clothing.

We never looked back. Just outside Libau we stopped for a moment and Lucy said the prayer for a safe trip and we thanked the Lord that we were able to make the trip back. It was a beautiful spring morning and the three of us were excited and eager to get on with it. We sang, we told jokes and we were happy. After a couple of hours we slowed down. The road was going through the mountains. There was neither traffic nor houses to be seen. It began to rain and then to pour. We walked on as best we could, but we didn't see any shelter around. Soon after the rain started, we were drenched to the skin and worried that our food was getting wet. It was a long way back home.

After a while, a large farmhouse came into view on the left-hand side of the road. Five minutes later we arrived. We knock on the door. A man opens it, takes one look at us and wants to slam the door shut, but we won't let him. Please, good man, listen to us, we are displaced persons, we won't harm anybody. We were in a concentration camp and we're on our way back home. Please let us come in and dry up. The man called his wife and told her what we'd said. She looked us over in disbelief. We could hear children's voices in the background.

"Please let us in," I said. "We won't hurt your children. These two women are mothers too."

They let us in, but they didn't want the wheelbarrow in the house. We insisted; we were afraid to be separated from it. They weren't too happy having us there because they didn't trust us, but in spite of that they took good care of us.

The woman gave each of us a towel to put on while our clothing was drying on a line through the kitchen, where there was a fire. The clock said shortly after nine; we'd walked for four hours. We were very hungry and didn't want to start on our bread, so we asked for breakfast. While the woman was preparing the food, the man wanted to know where we were going and where we'd been in the war. We told him that as soon as our clothes were dry and the rain had stopped we were heading to the butcher in Trutnow and that was all for the first day. We each got a couple of eggs, sunny side up, and a big piece of bread with butter, and milk. These were our first eggs, delicious, even tastier than I remembered. The rain didn't stop, and the farmer wanted to get rid of us. He seemed afraid to have us in the house too long.

A man came into the house to do some business with the farmer. He was also fed. While he was eating, he noticed us in the corner. Only then did the farmer tell him about us. The man told us he had a truck outside and he was driving to Trutnow anyway. He didn't mind dropping us off somewhere. Yes, he knew the butcher.

"Everybody knows the butcher in Trutnow," he told us.

By the time the man was ready to leave, our clothes were dry. His truck turned out to be very old with an open back. We got in the back with our wheelbarrow, and because the rain hadn't let up, we were covered with a large canvas. After a bumpy ride, the truck stopped, and when we came out from under the canvas, the rain had stopped and the sun was shining.

All the people who helped us seemed to have one thing in common. They were afraid somebody might see what they did. The truck-driver left us in the middle of a street and said that he had to leave. The butcher was only a few blocks away. He took off so fast we couldn't even say thank you.

Trutnow looked like a bigger town than Libau. We saw some nice houses with gardens in front. The spring flowers were blooming and seemed to be welcoming us to Czechoslovakia. It was only a short walk to the butcher shop. We looked through the shop window and saw several people inside the store. We hesitated a moment and then stepped inside. Three undernourished ragged women with a wheelbarrow, no wonder the man had a bewildered look on his face when we walked in. We greeted everyone in a friendly way, and Netty handed the butcher the letter from his friend in Libau.

The butcher read the letter and said he was very happy to hear from his friend again. He looked a little puzzled at what his friend had sent him. He asked us what we wanted, and before we could say a word we were pushed into a room behind the store. His wife and daughter were in the room, both of them terribly shocked at the sight of us. The butcher told his wife the contents of the letter we'd brought him. I watched their faces while they were talking to each other. They were horrified. We assured them we had no intention of staying in their house one minute longer than necessary. We wanted to get on as soon as possible.

They told us there was a railroad station in town, but no trains had gone yet because there had been fighting in Prague. We could stay in their house if we didn't go into the shop. They'd give us the master bedroom, which had twin beds. Would we please stay upstairs?

Because I was still very much bothered by lice, we decided that I was going to get one of the big beds by myself, and Netty and Lucy would share the other one. As soon as I'd seen the room, I went back downstairs and started to talk to the daughter of the house, who was in her early teens and thought it very interesting and exciting to talk to me. I convinced her she should go with me to the railroad station because I wanted to find out when the trains would start going again. Until now, we'd never even thought about a train; all we had thought about was walking.

The girl had to ask her mother's permission. She said

yes so long as we didn't walk next to each other on the street. Otherwise people would talk about her. Away we went to the station, which wasn't far at all. On the way, even though we weren't walking next to each other, the girl started to talk to me. She said we shouldn't be angry that her parents were so afraid to have us, but because they were Sudeten Germans and Germany had lost the war, they didn't want to make any wrong moves.

The girl was a great help to me at the station because the man at the wicket refused to listen to me speaking German, and I couldn't speak Czech. I found out that the fighting in Prague had stopped the Friday before and that sometime soon the trains would go again.

We went back to the butcher's house, where supper was waiting for me upstairs in the bedroom. We had had a good day. We were in Trutnow, with a chance of taking a train to Prague, and we hadn't used much of our food.

After supper we went to sleep in our deep feather beds. As usual we woke up at daybreak, and right away I set out to go to the station with the girl. She thought it was silly to go so early, but I was determined that we'd be on the first train to Prague. Again the girl spoke to the people at the station for me, and from that conversation, I had the feeling that first train wouldn't be too far off.

I told Lucy and Netty about my findings, and we decided that we would go back again in a couple of hours. After a good breakfast, Netty and I went. I was amazed to see the difference there. It had become a busy meeting-place with people running around and talking. We had a hard time finding out what was going on. The people didn't want to speak German. Finally somebody said a special train for VIPs was leaving at noon, but nobody knew if the train would be able to reach Prague.

That was all we needed to know. We ran back to the

butcher's house, told Lucy the good news and asked the woman to pack us a lunch. I watched her make beautiful sandwiches with real cold meat. We thanked them for all their hospitality and, with our wheelbarrow still full, we went to the station.

We weren't a minute too soon. The train wasn't going to leave at noon, but at 10.30 AM. No, no, you women can't go on the train, the conductor told us. This train is for VIPs only. That was fine with us, we were VIPs, and we had important papers from the Russians to prove it. We waved the paper in front of him. He took a look at it. Probably he understood it as little as we did.

"Yes, you can go on the train," he said. "All you need is tickets."

"No, didn't you read the paper?" we asked. "The paper says the tickets are paid for."

"Well, hurry and get into the train," the conductor said. "But we really have no room for that wheelbarrow."

"Sorry sir, but the wheelbarrow goes where we go. It's our baggage."

We went into the train. I couldn't believe it was true. On the way to Prague, like free human beings. The train was very full, standing-room only. I had a hard time finding room for our wheelbarrow.

Soon we started to eat an early lunch, then a lunch and then a late lunch. In the meantime the train advanced very slowly. It came to a halt after a little while, and everybody was told to change trains.

Out of the train with the wheelbarrow and over the tracks to another train. This same scene was repeated several times. Finally we got seats in a compartment, and a man started to talk to me. A completely new experience for me, and also for him. He was seeing survivors from the concentration camps for the first time. I told him a little bit about our trip. The man was from Prague, and he was very kind and helpful. He told us that near the railroad station in Prague there was an information booth set up to help the displaced persons who were coming from all over Eastern Europe. We should go there, and he was sure we'd get shelter somewhere in the city. He also wanted to know how we'd paid for the trip. We proudly showed him the paper we had from the Russian. He could read Russian, but he didn't say anything. He just sat there with a big grin on his face. He advised us very firmly to get rid of the wheelbarrow before we got to Prague. We ate some more, and started to split up the food and put it in our bags.

The man gave us some money and his telephone number in Prague, in case we needed help. We greatly appreciated his kindness; it was such a new experience to be spoken to as an equal human being. This man was truly happy for us, that we'd survived the war.

We arrived in Prague in the early evening, said good-bye to our new friend and parted with our wheelbarrow. I felt a certain loss. Outside the station was the information booth for displaced people. We took our place in the lineup. After only a couple of questions, we received some food and a map with directions to the place where we'd be staying. It was a long walk. We walked all the way up Wenzel Square, and I was very impressed with what a beautiful city Prague was.

The address we'd been given turned out to be a high school. The classrooms had been transformed into large dormitories with cots side by side. The basement had a dining-room. That was welcome news.

We were shown to cots without any questions asked. All we were told was to check in next morning with the doctor, whose office was on the second floor.

We ate some of our bread and started to talk to the other people. We didn't talk about the past and avoided mention of anything to do with the war. We were still mainly interested in two things, where to get food and how to get back quickly. I think we were afraid to ask any of the people which camp they'd been in and who they'd met and if they knew who'd survived. We weren't yet ready to face the truth.

Breakfast in the building was served at 8 AM, but we'd already eaten some of our bread as we had no intention of letting it go to waste or of missing any opportunity to get a meal.

The doctor turned out to be himself a survivor from a camp. He was a young man in his early thirties who'd lost his wife and a young child. He told us that at certain places in the city breakfast was served to displaced persons. We also learned that the Netherlands had no representative in Prague and that we'd be informed who'd be in charge of us. The days of no official papers or identification were over. After being only a number, it was nice to be known by name again.

We went to investigate the city. The streetcars were free for us; we showed our number and that took care of the fare. We noticed a street-corner where food was handed out. At the next stop, we left the streetcar and walked back to the free food stand. They told us that at seven in the morning we could come for boiled eggs and that there were foodstands on several corners. It didn't take us long to find them. We met other people from the building where we were housed, also eating away.

Later on, we were to meet a young Dutchman who was in charge of getting together the people who wanted to go west. He was cute, and I got a crush on him. He told us that the Swedish consulate was going to give us papers, but we had to go to the consulate as soon as possible. Our busy schedule of eating left us some time to go and see the Swedes.

The next morning after our rounds, first breakfast with eggs, then breakfast at our place, we took the public transportation to the Swedish consulate, which was located in one of the most attractive districts of Prague. The Swedes were very friendly and helpful and asked only a few questions. They told us we needed a passport photo and then they could give us our papers. We left the consulate wondering where we could get our pictures taken. We didn't really want to see a picture of ourselves. A few blocks down the hill, we noticed a sign on a door, Photographer. We rang the bell, and a man opened the door. We explained to him what we needed the pictures for. He took a picture of each of us and said he'd have them ready the next day. The price was 50 kronen each for three pictures.

"But we only have 50 kronen together. We don't want three pictures each. All we want is one."

He said that he never made less than three pictures, and the price was 50 kronen each and if we wanted the photos we had better have the money. We tried to get him to have some sympathy with our situation, but he wouldn't change his mind.

Strolling in the sunshine, we tried to think of what to do next. A nun in her full habit came walking toward us. We stopped her and I told her our story. The sister reached into her pocket and gave us 20 kronen.

Now we'd become street beggars. Well, no time to lose. A middle-aged man in a good-fitting suit walked toward us. We stopped him and told him our story. He didn't say a word, just opened his wallet and gave us 100 kronen and walked quickly on. Now we were the owners of 170 kronen, and we'd be able to pay for the photos the next day.

Life was really good to us that day. On the next corner we noticed a beggar standing with his hat in front of him. We gave him 10 kronen.

The next day we went proudly to the photographer with our 150 kronen. The pictures were waiting for us, and before we could do or say anything, the photographer said that he'd thought about us all night, and he wanted only 50 kronen for the photos. We paid, thanked him and were on the way to the Swedes for our papers.

As soon as we came back from our trip to the Swedish consulate, we learned that the Prague police intended to supply us with some kind of identification and a permit to stay in the city of Prague. In order to get the papers, we had to go to the city hall, which was located in a beautiful old square. We received our "acknowledgment" from the police and were told to come back for food stamps and money. Two days later, the bank of Prague gave every one of the displaced persons 1000 kronen. Now we wanted to spend our money, but the stores in Prague were still closed. They hadn't reopened since the end of the war.

Every day I had a little visit with the doctor, and after several friendly talks, I finally had the courage to tell him that I was terribly bothered by lice. The doctor immediately made the necessary arrangements for me to go to a delousing centre the very next day. None too soon, for the parasites were driving me crazy.

I got a map with directions and the numbers of the streetcars I had to take. It turned out to be a long trip. The delousing centre looked like a factory. After I rang the bell, a man opened the door and said something in Czech. I told him in German I was sorry I didn't speak

Czech, that I was from Holland. I wished to be deloused.

What a thing to have to say.

The man, who was expecting me, let me in and told me to strip off all my clothes and give them to him. I gave him all my clothes and my coat.

"Didn't the doctor tell you to bring all your clothing with you to the centre?" he said.

"Of course he did," I replied. "I brought all my clothes."

"What about your nightclothing and underwear?"

"This is all the clothing I possess," I assured him.

I could see he wasn't really convinced. He directed me to a deep stone bathtub, which was filled with warm water and chemicals. I had to sit in it for a long time. Once in a while, the man would come and put more chemicals into the water. Then he told me to come out and dry myself with a towel he gave me. Then I got back my clothing, which had also been deloused.

When I was ready to leave, I wanted to pay the man. After all I was now a girl with money. He looked at me with pity and said "How could I take money from you?" The funny thing was that I didn't feel sorry for myself, or poor. I felt happy, grateful to be alive and deloused.

The trip had taken up almost a whole day. I couldn't wait to tell Lucy and Netty about my experience. They'd done some more exploring in the city and had come upon a health club where they had so much fun that they insisted I must visit it the next day.

The following day started like all the days in Prague, with a trip to all the stands that provided us with breakfast and then back to our own building for breakfast there. Next, a visit to the doctor and an attempt to find out when we'd be leaving. Probably toward the end of the week.

It wasn't difficult to find the health club. It was on one of the main streets, located in a large house. I rang the bell at the door of the club, paid the fee and marched in. For a few more kronen I got a large bath-towel and a bar of soap. I found the showers. What a pleasure to feel the warm water over my body for as long as I wanted! After the shower I looked around and noticed in the next room a couple of tables on which women were getting massaged. I was leaning against the doorpost watching, feeling like Alice in Wonderland. This couldn't be real. I stood for a while on the same spot, trying to take it all in. The masseuse asked me if I wanted a turn. Yes, please, I'd love to have a massage. I climbed on the table and the woman looked me over.

"I can't massage you," she said. "You're only bones and I'm afraid I'd break you."

I had gained a pound every day while I was in Prague, and I thought I was getting fatter. I must have looked disappointed because the woman said "Well okay, I can give you a little massage."

After she finished I climbed off the table and started to pay her.

"I couldn't take any money from you," she said.

How was I ever going to get rid of my money?

"Thank you," I said and went on to the next room.

The next room was very large. Again I found myself in the doorway, looking in and wondering if I was dreaming. This place looked like the pictures of ancient Rome in my high-school history book, with the naked matrons sitting around the marble pool gossiping.

Here some of the women were playing in the round pool. Others were talking. I thought about going for a swim but decided against it and just stood there watching the women and looking into a different world.

All that first week, we'd noticed a grim expression on the faces of many of the people of Prague. The war, the many years of German occupation, had left their mark on everybody. Then on the weekend we witnessed, with thousands of others, the entry of Mr. Benes and his troops into the city. As the people waved their flags and banners, the smiles seemed to be returning to their faces. It was a very impressive spectacle, an enormous contrast with my life of the past few years. It was like a vacation before facing a new chapter of life.

My body wasn't used to the regular food yet, and I was still very much bothered by diarrhea. One thing we'd never been able to find out was whether the city had any public washrooms we could use. Often I had to rush back to the residence from somewhere in the city. Since the streetcar didn't go all the way, we had a little walk from the streetcar stop. On one occasion I knew I couldn't make it all the way back. On the top of Wentzler Place fighting had gone on till shortly before we came to Prague, and several large piles of debris were still untouched. I decided to make use of the ruins. Nobody knew me, and I didn't know anybody.

But when I was finished and walked away from my hiding-place, the only person in Prague I didn't want to see me was there. The young Dutchman who was in charge of transportation passed by and noticed me. After that encounter, I never talked to the man again.

By Wednesday evening of our second week in Prague, we'd been informed that our departure would be on Friday morning. A trainload of people would be leaving for the west. We should be at the railroad station at a certain time with our papers. This was much sooner than we'd hoped for. Thursday we spent eating, investigating the railroad station and making one last tour of Prague.

The goodbyes in Prague were not too many. I thanked the doctor who had been very nice to me. We had spent some pleasant hours talking to each other. He'd even offered me a chocolate bar, but my stomach wasn't ready for that yet.

At the railroad station, Lucy, Netty and I stuck together as always, watching out for each other. Apparently the Russians were in charge of the first part of the trip, which was going to take us to Pilsen. In Pilsen we would somehow be delivered to the Americans.

The trip to Pilsen, which is a relatively short distance from Prague, took many hours, but we had plenty of food and a whole life ahead of us. In the middle of the afternoon, we were let out on the platform at Pilsen with the message that the Americans would look after us from now on. The Russians left Pilsen immediately.

After a while a small number of American soldiers showed up. It was nice to see these good-looking young men in clean uniforms, and for the first time I noticed faces that looked genuinely happy.

Transportation to the next place wasn't yet available, but we were generously supplied with food, this time from American army rations. Nobody seemed to know when the trucks that were going to take us into Germany would arrive, so we were advised to find a place to sleep in one of the boxcars or on the platform. No sooner were we settled down in one of the boxcars than the insects came out of every conceivable corner and started to attack us. It had only been a few days since I was deloused, and now this again. We returned to the platform.

With the soldiers around us, it seemed as if we were back under guard, but these boys were our friends. We asked them what was going on in the world and where we were going next. The soldier I talked to most was wearing four big watches. He asked what he could do for me.

"You could give me one of your watches," I said.

"Sure," he said, "but you have to go with me so I can show you Pilsen."

"No thank you. I don't need to see Pilsen. I don't need your watch."

Netty, Lucy and I spent the whole night lying on the platform under a clear sky. The next morning we heard that trucks would be coming for us sometime during the day and that we'd be taken to the city of Bamberg in Germany.

We'd spent 24 hours at the station before the Americans arrived with big open trucks. In no time at all we were loaded into the trucks and away we went. Everybody told me what a beautiful breathtaking trip it was through the mountains. I slept through the whole trip and didn't see a thing. I didn't care.

I was discouraged now, and angry when I found out that the Americans had put us, "for our own protection," in a military compound in Bamberg. After the taste of freedom in Prague, I had a terribly hard time accepting the fact of being cooped up again. The place was heavily guarded by US soldiers, and we weren't allowed outside the grounds. I don't know if the soldiers were protecting us from the Germans or the Germans from us. Another thing that didn't improve my mood was hearing from the Dutch survivors who arrived each day, the many, many names of those who were dead.

I was so anxious to get back to Tilburg, but I had to have patience. We were told it would probably be as much as two weeks before the next transport departure to the Netherlands.

As usual I was lucky. An unexpectedly large number

of Dutch survivors was arriving in Bamberg each day, so a train had to be found to ship us out and make room for the people from other countries and the ones who had no country to go back to. Many of the arrivals were in very poor health and needed medical attention really desperately.

Several boxcars were found for us for the trip to the Netherlands and Belgium. The cars were lined with plenty of clean fresh straw. Not too many people were assigned to each car; one had enough room to stretch out and sleep. The US army supplied us with enough rations to satisfy us, which meant a lot of food. We had boxcars, we had food, we were relatively comfortable, what we needed now was a locomotive to pull us. However this was 1945 in postwar Germany, and hardware wasn't easy to come by. What was available was in use by the armies for troop transport.

Finally our boxcars were joined to a long train which was going in the right direction, but after a couple of hours, for some reason or no reason, we were taken off again. We were sitting in the middle of nowhere, but unlike our previous boxcar rides, we had the door open, and when we were stopped, we could jump out and do some investigating. After several hours of waiting, we were pulled forward in the right direction for a while. The same pattern was repeated many times until, around 11 o'clock on Sunday night the tenth of June, the train arrived in Roermond in the Netherlands.

We were most cordially and warmly received by some officials. Again we were directed to a building in which we could shelter through the night. After a midnight snack, we were told that the next morning, as soon as we were cleared by the border customs for security and health, we would be free to go where we wanted.

Neither Lucy nor Netty had ever said anything to me about what to expect or what to do after my return. This last night, they advised me that if I should be left without my parents, I shouldn't get married on the rebound or in a hurry. I should keep my head.

I had one bad nightmare after another, so I decided to get up and try to be one of the first to go through security. I went outside for some fresh air and to have a good look around. Suddenly I heard a voice calling my name. Before I knew what was going on, someone had taken me in his arms and was telling me how glad he was that I'd returned. It was Jules Goldschmid, a boy I'd attended Jewish high school with during the war. He lived not too far away from the building where I'd spent the night, and he'd come early to see if he knew any of the arrivals and if he could be of any help to them. He said he'd be waiting for me to get through.

I was one of the first inside the customs building, but soon everybody else seemed to be just as eager as I was to get it over with. The doctor didn't like my cough. Neither did I. He wanted me to have X-rays after I got back to Tilburg. Everything went smoothly, and the officials were kind and understanding. At the exit stood a person who asked us if we were single or married. The singles got one guilder and a married person received two guilders and fifty cents. I couldn't understand why a married person who was just as alone as I was should get more than I did.

Jules was waiting for me. I said goodbye to my dear friends Lucy and Netty, not a long emotional goodbye, just a handshake and so long.

Jules told me that most of the bridges over the rivers in the Netherlands had been destroyed. He'd take me as far as Eindhoven, and then he'd go back. In Roermond we had to cross the river in a barge with me hidden under some boxes. Later we hitch-hiked to Helmond and to Eindhoven where I was to catch a train. I went to the ticket office and discovered a ticket to Tilburg was two guilders. I was single and had only my one guilder. Thank goodness Jules was still around. "Don't worry," he said and bought me the ticket.

The train was a passenger train, not a boxcar. It was one of those with compartments with closed doors and a corridor along the side. I stood in the corridor, feeling shy and out of place. Someone asked me something, but my mind was so preoccupied that I didn't understand the question. A while later another person came and said very kindly to me "There's a seat for you inside the compartment. Do come and sit down."

I still wasn't completely sure that I wanted to sit with everybody. Too many feelings inside me, hope, expectation and apprehension. Who would I find at Doortje's house? That was to be the meeting-place for our family.

The people around me were chatting away, but I didn't pay any attention until I heard a lady across from me say, "Aren't you Miss Roos from the Nieuwe Bosscheweg?"

"Yes," I said, "yes." Hoping for good news.

"Well," the lady said, "I live opposite your parents' house. I'm glad to see you coming back. Why didn't you let us know you were coming on the train today? We would have had a band at the station to welcome you back home."

"Thank you very much," I said, "but I really didn't know when I'd be coming back."

The train was getting nearer to Tilburg, and I could see the familiar landmarks. One of the first was the Church of the Sacraments, which looked quite heavily damaged. It gave me a peculiar awareness that everybody and everything had some scars left from this dreadful war.

In the railroad station, there was lots going on, but I didn't stay any longer than it took to show my repatriation papers to an official, who told me to come back the next day or so and get my ration coupons and register at the town hall.

I was free to go.

With my little bag under my arm, I walked as fast as I could to my friend Doortje's house, a twenty-minute walk. I didn't give myself a chance to look around too much.

During the war, when I used to visit the Evertse house, I'd ring the bell three times so Doortje and her mother knew it was me calling.

I found myself giving the bell the same three short rings. Mrs. Evertse opened the door and said, "Hello Anita," just as if she had just seen me the day before.

"Look Doortje, who is here."

Doortje came running quickly to the door.

"Oh good, you're back again. Oh are you skinny," she cried out. "Are you the only one who came back?"

I looked over Doortje's shoulder into the empty living-room and said, with a little difficulty, "I guess so."